Fresh Ways with
Lamb

COVER
A sweet-sour fig sauce enhances lightly grilled noisettes (recipe, page 31). Taken from the loin, one of the leanest cuts of lamb, noisettes are an optimal choice for the health-conscious cook.

TIME-LIFE BOOKS

EUROPEAN EDITOR: Ellen Phillips
Design Director: Ed Skyner
Director of Editorial Resources: Louise Tulip
Chief Sub-Editor: Ilse Gray

LOST CIVILIZATIONS
HOW THINGS WORK
SYSTEM EARTH
LIBRARY OF CURIOUS AND UNUSUAL FACTS
BUILDING BLOCKS
A CHILD'S FIRST LIBRARY OF LEARNING
VOYAGE THROUGH THE UNIVERSE
THE THIRD REICH
MYSTERIES OF THE UNKNOWN
TIME-LIFE HISTORY OF THE WORLD
FITNESS, HEALTH AND NUTRITION
HEALTHY HOME COOKING
UNDERSTANDING COMPUTERS
THE ENCHANTED WORLD
LIBRARY OF NATIONS
PLANET EARTH
THE GOOD COOK
THE WORLD'S WILD PLACES

HEALTHY HOME COOKING

SERIES DIRECTOR: Jackie Matthews
Studio Stylist: Liz Hodgson
Editorial Assistant: Eugénie Romer

Editorial Staff for *Fresh Ways with Lamb:*
Editor: Neil Fairbairn
Researcher: Heather Campion
Designer: Mike Snell
Sub-Editor: Christine Noble

PICTURE DEPARTMENT:
Administrator: Patricia Murray
Picture Co-ordinator: Amanda Hindley

EDITORIAL PRODUCTION:
Chief: Maureen Kelly
Assistant: Samantha Hill
Editorial Department: Theresa John, Debra Lelliott

THE CONTRIBUTORS

JOANNA BLYTHMAN is a cook and recipe writer who owns a specialist food shop in Edinburgh. She contributes articles on cookery to a number of newspapers and trade periodicals.

SILVIJA DAVIDSON studied at Leith's School of Food and Wine and specializes in the development of recipes from Latvia and other international cuisines.

JOANNA FARROW, a home economist and recipe writer who contributes regularly to food magazines, is especially interested in decorative presentation of food. Her books include *Creative Cake Decorating* and *Novelty Cakes for Children.*

JENI WRIGHT is a freelance cookery writer and editor with wide ranging culinary interests. Among the books she has written are *French Cooking, Midday Meals* and *Entertaining with Friends.*

The following also contributed recipes to this volume: Maddalena Bonino, Heather Campion, Alexandra Carlier, Yvonne Hamlett, Carole Handslip, Pam Howe, Antony Kwok, Hilary Newstead, Jane Suthering.

THE COOKS

The recipes in this book were cooked for photography by Pat Alburey, Allyson Birch, Jane Bird, Jill Eggleton, Joanna Farrow, Carole Handslip, Janice Murfitt, Jane Suthering.
Studio Assistant: Rita Walters.

CONSULTANT

PAT ALBUREY is a home economist with a wide experience of preparing foods for photography, teaching cookery and creating recipes. She has written a number of cookery books and she was the studio consultant for the Time-Life series *The Good Cook.* In addition to acting as the general consultant on this volume, she also created a number of the recipes.

NUTRITION CONSULTANT

PATRICIA JUDD trained as a dietician and worked in hospital practice before returning to university to obtain her MSc and PhD degrees. For the last 12 years she has lectured in Nutrition and Dietetics at London University.

Nutritional analyses for *Fresh Ways with Lamb* were derived from McCance and Widdowson's *The Composition of Food* by A.A. Paul and D.A.T. Southgate, and other current data.

This volume is one of a series of illustrated cookery books that emphasize the preparation of healthy dishes for today's weight-conscious, nutrition-minded eaters.

Fresh Ways with Lamb

BY

THE EDITORS OF TIME-LIFE BOOKS

TIME-LIFE BOOKS/AMSTERDAM

Contents

Lamb and Broccoli Stir-Fry

Chilled Cutlets Coated with Mint Aspic

Moroccan Spiced Stew

Port Paupiettes

Diced Lamb with Pink Grapefruit and Tarragon

3 Inspired Combinations 89

4 Microwaving Lamb 123

Techniques 134

Salade Niçoise

A New Approach to Lamb

Over the millennia no meat has more regularly graced the tables of mankind than lamb. It was some 10,000 years ago that tribesmen in Central Asia first domesticated sheep for their meat, milk and wool. By 7,000 B.C. the pastoral way of life had become widespread throughout the Middle East, where flocks of hardy sheep thrived despite punishing extremes of heat and cold. Little wonder that sheep are the first domestic animal mentioned in the Bible. Adam's son Abel, we learn in Genesis, was ''a keeper of sheep'', and when he made a sacrifice to God, he chose to offer up his new-born lambs.

During its association with mankind, the sheep has even-handedly fed both the rich and the poor. In many parts of the world its meat has long been served for feasting and holy days, but equally for everyday fare. In medieval Europe, the servant who carried the roast saddle of lamb, crisp and golden, to the banqueting table, returned to the kitchen for his own bowl of mutton stew — not such an imposing dish as his master's but just as nutritious and full of flavour. Throughout the Islamic Middle East, a whole roast lamb is still the centrepiece of wedding feasts and other festivities, while lesser cuts play a central role in most ordinary meat dishes.

In other parts of the prosperous modern world, however, this most democratic of providers has lost its pride of place in many kitchens. Beef and pork, as well as poultry such as chicken, are today all produced inexpensively enough to compete with lamb at the table. A further blow to the prestige of lamb comes from health-conscious cooks who are wary of the fat content of red meats in general, and who regard lamb as having only a limited place in a healthy diet.

This volume aims to restore lamb to its rightful place as a food for everyman. Reflecting its classless appeal, the 114 recipes offer inspiration for every kind of occasion, summer or winter. There are simple chops and cutlets, grand roasts, subtly flavoured stews, assemblages of meat and vegetables, sautés and salads. Devised by Time-Life Books' own team of chefs and nutritionists, these dishes have been prepared with a minimum

of fat and oil, allowing the most health-conscious cooks to choose freely from among them.

A nutritional profile

By any standards, lamb, like other red meats, is a highly nutritious food. A single 90 g (3 oz) serving of cooked lamb provides about 20 g (¾ oz) of valuable animal protein — one third of the total daily intake recommended for adults. Just as beneficial is the range of vitamins present in red meat. Lamb is an important source of B vitamins, essential for a healthy skin and nervous system. A 90 g (3 oz) serving, for example, contains over 40 per cent of the adult male's recommended daily intake of niacin and of vitamin B_{12}. Lamb is also rich in iron, in the form known as ''haem iron'', which is not only easily absorbed by the body, but also promotes the absorption of iron from other foods.

The major drawback of lamb as part of a healthy diet is its high fat content. Most people are aware that we eat too much fat for our own well-being. Indeed, nutritionists urge us to cut our total fat consumption by about one quarter — from nearly 40 per cent of our daily energy intake to about 30 per cent. They are especially insistent on the wisdom of cutting down on saturated fats — contained in animal fats — which promote the production of cholesterol in the body. Although cholesterol is produced naturally by the liver and in small amounts contributes to good health, excessive production stimulated by a diet high in saturated fats can, over a period of time, lead to heart disease.

Fortunately, lamb is a less fatty meat than it used to be. European farmers, encouraged by consumer demand and, in the U.K., by agricultural subsidies, are generally producing leaner lamb than was available a few years ago. In any case, most of the fat found in a cut of lamb can easily be trimmed off before cooking. But lean, uncooked lamb still contains about 9 per cent intramuscular fat. This proportion is slightly higher than is found in pork, and about twice as much as is present in lean beef. In other words, a certain intake of saturated fat cannot be avoided when you sit down to a dish of lamb. You would not want it otherwise, for fat in reasonable measure contributes to the flavour and succulence of meat; it is one of the reasons why lamb has been so highly regarded for so long.

The healthy strategy adopted by the authors of this volume is to prepare the meat so that it is as fat-free as possible, and to eliminate all unnecessary fats from the cooking process, using the much more benign polyunsaturated or monounsaturated fats where necessary. An upper limit of 14 g total fat per 90 g (3 oz) serving of cooked lamb has been imposed as a reasonable guideline. These recipes also limit salt to no more than 400 mg per portion, since a high salt intake is also implicated in heart disease. At the same time, Time-Life Books' team of cooks and nutrition experts have in no way compromised the unique flavour and texture of lamb.

Choosing, buying and storing

A recommended first step in buying good-quality lean lamb is to seek the advice of a knowledgeable butcher. He should be able to tell you the age and origin of the animal — factors that influence the appearance, flavour and fat content of the meat. As a general rule, the younger the lamb the paler and less fatty the meat. Lowland breeds are not inherently leaner than hill breeds, but they gain weight faster and are usually slaughtered at an earlier age. A fresh spring lamb of about six months has rose-pink flesh and white, firm fat; brittle, chalk-white fat suggests that the meat has been frozen. Certain hill breeds, however, have darker flesh than lowland strains, as does meat that has been hung. A useful indicator of a lamb's age is its bones; in a young animal they have a pinkish-blue tinge, while in older animals they are white and less pliant.

There is no general agreement as to when lamb becomes mutton, for different breeds mature at different rates. It is safe to say, however, that an animal is no longer sold as lamb after it is a year old. Of course, mutton is now something of a rarity in Europe, being found mainly in butcher's shops which cater for Asian or Middle Eastern communities.

Although the emphasis in this volume is on lean cuts, the recipes also make use of cuts from most other parts of the carcass. Not included are recipes for the breast and the middle and scrag end of neck (the section nearest the head), which have a very high fat content, even after trimming. The liver, although a rich source of vitamin A, has a cholesterol content that exceeds the limit prescribed for healthy diets, and should only be eaten occasionally. Shoulder of lamb appears infrequently in the recipes; full of flavour but also high in fat, this cut requires meticulous trimming before it is cooked.

The principal source of lean meat on a lamb is the fillet end — the wide upper section — of the leg. Cuts from the fillet can be cubed for stews and kebabs, minced for meat loaf and kofta, or sliced and pounded flat to create lamb's answer to the veal escalope, ideal for quick grilling or flash-frying. The best end of neck and the loin — adjacent cuts along the back of the carcass — yield smaller pieces of extremely tender lean meat. The best end, whether roasted whole as a rack or separated into individual cutlets, should be carefully trimmed of fat so that only the "eye" of lean meat along the backbone remains. Likewise, the loin can be cut into chops and trimmed of fat, or boned to yield two strips of lean meat — the eye and the small but exquisitely tender fillet *(page 134)*.

Several of the preparatory techniques illustrated on pages 134 to 136 are tasks routinely undertaken by a butcher, whose work is time-saving and usually free. You can order ready-to-cook noisettes, for example, or a boned leg or loin. Alternatively, buy the basic cuts and prepare them for cooking yourself; no doubt your own efforts will be slow, but you can take satisfaction in removing every piece of surplus fat. Likewise, the leanest and freshest mince is obtained by chopping by hand at home.

Stored in the coolest part of the refrigerator, fresh lamb will keep without spoiling for up to three days. Remove its wrapping and place it on a rack above a plate to encourage the circulation of air. Cover it with an upturned bowl to prevent its surface from drying out. Minced lamb, however, should be eaten within two days of being refrigerated.

Lamb will keep in the freezer for six to nine months; minced lamb for four months. Freeze only fresh meat, extracting all air from the freezer bag or foil parcel before storing.

Appetizing flavours, healthy techniques

To keep fat and cholesterol levels within healthy limits the recipes that follow call for skimmed milk in place of whole milk and polyunsaturated margarine rather than butter. Cheese is used only as a topping, never a principal ingredient, while cream — that staple of the traditional rich sauce — finds a sumptuous but relatively low-fat replacement in thick Greek yogurt. To reduce both fat and calories, gravies and sauces are thickened with cornflour or arrowroot, rarely with the traditional *roux* made from plain flour and fat.

Far from limiting the variety and appeal of the recipes, these restrictions free a range of flavours that too often are suppressed by rich ingredients. Fibre-rich fresh vegetables and grains, dried fruits and pulses are traditional partners for lamb, and they are made full use of here. The reduced level of salt permits fresh herbs and spices to assert their flavours with refreshing clarity.

Cooking techniques are also tailored to meet the dietary guidelines. In Healthy Home Cooking's test kitchens, heavy-

The Key to Better Eating

Healthy Home Cooking addresses the concerns of today's weight-conscious, health-minded cooks with recipes developed within nutritional guidelines.

The chart *(right)* gives dietary guidelines for healthy men, women and children. Recommended figures vary from country to country, but the principles are the same everywhere. Here, the average daily amounts of calories and protein are from a report by the U.K. Department of Health and Social Security; the maximum advisable daily intake of fat is based on guidelines given by the National Advisory Committee on Nutrition Education (NACNE); those for cholesterol and sodium are based on upper limits suggested by the World Health Organization.

The volumes in the Healthy Home Cooking series do not purport to be diet books, nor do they focus on health foods. Rather, the books express a commonsense approach to cooking that uses salt, sugar, cream, butter and oil in moderation while including other ingredients that also contribute flavour and satisfaction. The portions themselves are modest in size.

The recipes make few unusual demands. Naturally they call for fresh ingredients, offering substitutes should these be unavailable. (Only the original ingredient is calculated in the nutrient analysis, however.) Most of the ingredients can be found in any well-stocked supermarket; the occasional exceptions can be bought in speciality or ethnic food shops.

Recommended Dietary Guidelines

		Average Daily Intake		Maximum Daily Intake			
		CALORIES	PROTEIN grams	CHOLESTEROL milligrams	TOTAL FAT grams	SATURATED FAT grams	SODIUM milligrams
Females	7-8	1900	47	300	80	32	2000*
	9-11	2050	51	300	77	35	2000
	12-17	2150	53	300	81	36	2000
	18-53	2150	54	300	81	36	2000
	54-74	1900	47	300	72	32	2000
Males	7-8	1980	49	300	80	33	2000
	9-11	2280	57	300	77	38	2000
	12-14	2640	66	300	99	44	2000
	15-17	2880	72	300	108	48	2000
	18-34	2900	72	300	109	48	2000
	35-64	2750	69	300	104	35	2000
	65-74	2400	60	300	91	40	2000

*(or 5g salt)

About cooking times.

To help the cook plan ahead effectively, Healthy Home Cooking takes time into account in all its recipes. While recognizing that everyone cooks at a different speed, and that stoves and ovens may differ somewhat in their temperatures, the series provides approximate "working" and "total" times for every dish. Working time stands for the minutes actively spent on preparation; total time includes unattended cooking time, as well as time devoted to marinating, steeping or soaking various ingredients. Because the recipes emphasize fresh foods, the dishes may take a bit longer to prepare than those in "quick and easy" cookery books that call for canned or packaged products, but the difference in flavour, and often in added nutritional value, should compensate for the little extra time involved.

bottomed pans are used to guard against burning the food when a small amount of oil is used. But non-stick pans brushed with the merest film of oil are perfectly adequate for browning meat and vegetables, as called for in many of the recipes. Safflower oil and virgin olive oil are favoured for sautéing. Safflower oil has been chosen because it is the most highly polyunsaturated oil generally available — and polyunsaturated vegetable fats are not only blameless in the cholesterol controversy, but may actually reduce the blood cholesterol level. A good second choice is sunflower oil, also high in polyunsaturated fats. Virgin olive oil is called for because it has a matchless fruity flavour and — like all olive oil — is high in monounsaturated fats, which are not linked to increased blood cholesterol levels. Lesser grades of olive oil, such as "pure", can be substituted for "virgin", though they lack its incomparable bouquet.

When cooked slowly in a liquid, even the leanest of lamb will release a small amount of fat. If the cooking liquid is to be used for a sauce or gravy, skim off the fat with a ladle or shallow spoon before serving. Alternatively, lay a paper towel flat on the surface, then lift it away immediately it has absorbed the layer of fat. A stew that is prepared in advance of a meal can be chilled and then degreased even more thoroughly simply by lifting off the solid layer of fat that collects at the surface.

Keeping low-fat cuts of meat moist is a particular problem when sautéeing, grilling or roasting. Denied the traditional techniques of basting or ladling the meat with extra fat, the health-conscious cook must adopt different strategies. One such method is to stuff a roast or chop with a savoury filling — such as the shoulder stuffed with wild rice and spinach on page 50 and the chops stuffed with walnuts and parsley on page 59 — that moisturize the meat from within as it cooks. Another technique, suitable for thin cuts of lamb, is to tenderize the meat in a marinade so that it cooks rapidly with a minimum wastage of moisture. Acidic marinades, made with vinegar, wine or citrus juices blended with aromatics, will break down the meat's fibres while imparting their own flavours. Treated in this way, a slice of fillet end of leg flattened with a meat bat will grill in very little time under a searing heat — and will taste all the better for the marriage of flavours.

Whatever techniques you use to keep lamb moist, prolonged exposure to dry heat will eventually desiccate the meat. For this reason, the range of cooking times recommended in the recipes are for rare to medium meat. If lamb that is still pink in the middle is not to your taste, add a minute or two to the cooking time for small pieces and 10 to 15 minutes for joints.

A choice of cooking methods.

Fresh Ways with Lamb is organized in four main chapters, each one devoted to a different cooking method. Chapter 1 deals with dry cooking methods — sautéing, grilling, roasting — and covers the simplest and quickest ways of cooking tender cuts. It also includes those grand conversation-stopping roasts of old-fashioned dinner parties: the saddle, the crown and the guard of honour. Chapter 2 describes moist cooking: braising, stewing and poaching. These methods, traditionally used to tenderize tougher cuts of lamb, have been adapted to give superb results with leaner cuts. Chapter 3 features assembled dishes, in which lamb is variously used as a stuffing for pastry and pancakes, extended with grains, pulses and pasta, layered with vegetables or tossed in salads. Finally, Chapter 4 describes ways of preparing lamb in a microwave oven, a quick, versatile cooking method.

Since many of the recipes call for unsalted brown or chicken stock, these recipes are given at the end of the book, together with a brief section on methods of preparing lamb for low-fat cooking, and a glossary of less familiar culinary terms and ingredients.

The ingredient list for each recipe starts with lamb and continues with the other ingredients in order of use. Both metric and imperial weights and volumes are given; the two sets of figures are not exact equivalents and should not be used together.

Like other volumes in this series, *Fresh Ways with Lamb* presents an analysis of nutrients contained in a single serving, plus approximate counts for calories, protein, cholesterol, total fat, saturated fat and sodium. In order to simplify meal planning, most recipes list suitable accompaniments. These are suggestions only; cooks should let their imagination guide them to achieving an appealing and sensible balance of foods.

Cuts of Lamb for Healthy Eating

This diagram shows major, or primal, cuts into which a lamb carcass is commonly divided by butchers. It also identifies the retail cuts called for by recipes in this book. With careful trimming, most parts of a lamb can provide low-fat meals. Only the breast and the middle and scrag end of neck are unacceptably fatty.

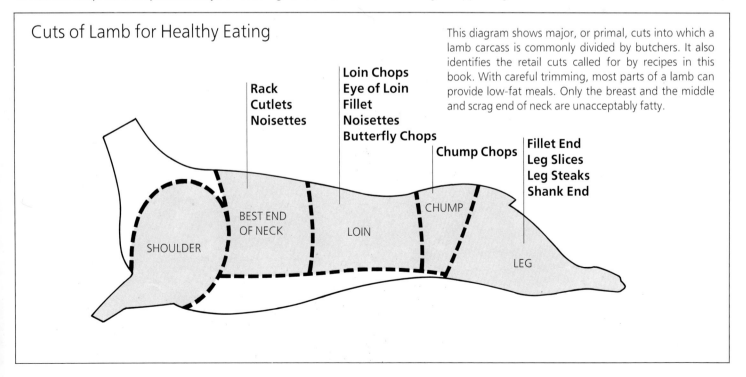

Rack
Cutlets
Noisettes

Loin Chops
Eye of Loin
Fillet
Noisettes
Butterfly Chops

Chump Chops

Fillet End
Leg Slices
Leg Steaks
Shank End

SHOULDER

BEST END OF NECK

LOIN

CHUMP

LEG

1 Lean strips of loin are stir-fried briefly in a wok with colourful fresh vegetables and a minimum of oil (recipe, page 22).

Updating the Classics

When Stone Age man first seared chunks of meat over an open fire, he inadvertently discovered one of the best methods of cooking. Today, barbecuing and grilling are as valued as ever for cooking many kinds of meat, including lamb. The benefits of grilling are allied to those of roasting and frying. All of these ''dry-cooking'' techniques use high heat to seal the meat's surface and trap the juices within. Together, they offer endless healthy, delicious ways of presenting lamb.

The choice of method depends partly upon the thickness and quality of the lamb. Tender strips of loin stir-fried in a sauté pan or traditional Chinese wok sear and cook through in little more than a minute. Thin cuts from the loin or best end of neck are well suited to the intense surface heat of grilling or frying, as are chops, cutlets and escalopes from the leg; anything much thicker may char on the outside before the inside has cooked sufficiently. Large cuts, such as racks, legs or shoulders, are generally roasted in the less intense overall heat of the oven. The tougher shank end of leg requires relatively slow roasting.

Because the heat of a grill, frying pan or oven can dry out and toughen meat, traditional recipes often call for lamb to be smeared with oil and basted with fat. The recipes in this chapter use a minimum of oil yet still achieve succulent results. Steeped in a marinade or flattened with a meat bat, slices of lamb become tender enough for rapid exposure to searing heat, while non-stick pans — merely brushed with oil — help break up the unhealthy alliance between frying and fat. Large cuts, such as the boned leg on page 49, can be stuffed with vegetables, which release their moisture during roasting. A moist coating on the outside of a joint also makes for tender meat: the rack on page 54 is roasted in its parsley marinade, which forms a protective crust and seals in the meat's juices.

Low-fat dry cooking does not mean that the showy Sunday roast is a thing of the past. When carefully trimmed, as demonstrated on page 135, even the normally fatty rack of lamb finds a place on the healthy menu. Well-trimmed racks can appear in traditional display pieces such as the guard of honour on page 55, while the crown roast on page 56 becomes a dish fit for a healthy king.

Several of the recipes that follow include a sauce made from the meat's roasting juices. While preparing the sauce the meat should be loosely covered with foil and kept warm. This resting period of 10 to 15 minutes allows the juices that have concentrated in the centre of the meat during cooking to flow back evenly throughout the joint, promoting firm, tender flesh and making carving easier.

Medallions with Watercress Sauce

Serves 4
Working time: about 35 minutes
Total time: about 45 minutes

Calories **200**
Protein **25g**
Cholesterol **90mg**
Total fat **11g**
Saturated fat **5g**
Sodium **90mg**

1 kg	loin of lamb, boned, trimmed of fat (page 134), eye cut diagonally into 12 slices, fillet reserved for another use	2¼ lb
30 cl	unsalted brown or chicken stock (recipes, page 137)	½ pint
2	bunches watercress, washed	2
4	fresh sage leaves, or ⅛ tsp dried sage	4
½ tsp	salt	½ tsp
	white pepper	
1 tbsp	apple jelly	1 tbsp
1 tbsp	Worcester sauce, mixed with 1 tbsp water	1 tbsp
1 tbsp	fromage frais	1 tbsp

To make the watercress sauce, boil the stock until the liquid is reduced by half — 5 to 10 minutes. Strip the leaves from the watercress, reserving four sprigs for garnish, and add the watercress and sage leaves to the reduced boiling stock. Cook the stock for a further 1 minute, allow it to cool slightly, then purée it in a blender or food processor. Transfer it to a small pan, season with half of the salt and some pepper and add the apple jelly. Stir the sauce over low heat until the jelly has melted, then remove the pan from the heat.

Season the lamb slices with the remaining ¼ teaspoon of salt and some pepper. Lightly brush a large non-stick frying pan with oil and brown six of the slices over high heat for 1 minute on each side. Reduce the heat to medium, add half of the Worcester sauce mixture and cook for a further 30 seconds to 1 minute on each side for rare to medium meat. Transfer the meat to a platter and keep it warm. Cook the remaining slices in the same way.

Heat the watercress sauce through, then remove it from the heat and stir in the *fromage frais*. Serve the lamb with the sauce, garnished with the reserved sprigs of watercress.

SUGGESTED ACCOMPANIMENT: *steamed button mushrooms.*

Flambéed Cutlets with Stuffed Apricots

Serves 4
Working time: about 40 minutes
Total time: about 6 hours and 50 minutes
(includes soaking and marinating)

Calories **260**
Protein **31g**
Cholesterol **75mg**
Total fat **8g**
Saturated fat **4g**
Sodium **175mg**

8	best end of neck cutlets (about 90 g/ 3 oz each), trimmed of fat	8
2 tbsp	coarsely chopped fresh ginger root	2 tbsp
2	garlic cloves, coarsely chopped	2
1	small onion, coarsely chopped	1
15 cl	fresh orange juice	¼ pint
¼ tsp	virgin olive oil	¼ tsp
125 g	mushrooms, finely chopped	4 oz
¼ tsp	salt	¼ tsp
	freshly ground black pepper	
8	dried whole apricots, soaked in water for 6 hours, or overnight	8
2 tbsp	brandy	2 tbsp
	parsley, for garnish (optional)	

Place the cutlets in a single layer in a shallow dish or casserole. Blend together the ginger, garlic, half the chopped onion and the orange juice in a food processor. Spoon the purée over the cutlets, cover loosely and leave them to marinate for at least 6 hours, or overnight, turning them once.

Heat the oil in a heavy frying pan. Add the mushrooms and the remaining onion, season them with half the salt and some pepper and sauté over medium heat until they are soft — 2 to 3 minutes.

Dry the apricots on paper towels and fill them with the mushroom and onion stuffing, enlarging the hole from which the stone was removed if necessary.

Remove the cutlets from the marinade and pat them dry with paper towels; strain the marinade and reserve it. Preheat a non-stick sauté pan and sear the cutlets for 1 minute on each side. Add the brandy and light it with a taper. When the flame dies down, arrange the stuffed apricots in the pan, pour in half of the marinade and sprinkle with the remaining salt. Cover with a tight-fitting lid and cook over low heat until the juices are still slightly pink when the cutlet is pierced with a knife — about 10 minutes.

Arrange the meat and stuffed apricots on a warm platter. Skim off any fat from the juices in the pan, then add the remaining marinade, bring it to the boil and simmer for 1 minute. Spoon the sauce over the lamb and serve, garnished, if you like, with parsley.

SUGGESTED ACCOMPANIMENTS: *French beans; steamed new potatoes.*

Medallions in Sweet-and-Sour Sauce

Serves 4
Working (and total) time: about 40 minutes

Calories **305**
Protein **26g**
Cholesterol **85mg**
Total fat **14g**
Saturated fat **6g**
Sodium **165mg**

1	rack of lamb (about 850 g/1¾ lb), boned (page 136, Steps 1 to 4), the fatty flap of meat that extends from the eye removed	1
20	shallots	20
20 g	unsalted butter	¾ oz
2 tbsp	red wine	2 tbsp
2 tsp	clear honey	2 tsp
½ tsp	salt	½ tsp
	freshly ground black pepper	
	chopped spring onions, for garnish	
Sweet-and-sour sauce		
200 g	young carrots	7 oz
200 g	young pink rhubarb	7 oz
10 cm	piece fresh ginger root	4 inch
¼ litre	red wine	8 fl oz
4 tbsp	finely chopped shallots	4 tbsp
60 cl	unsalted brown stock (recipe, page 137)	1 pint
1 tsp	clear honey	1 tsp

Start by preparing the ingredients for the sauce. Cut half the carrots and rhubarb into 6 cm by 3 mm (2½ by ⅛ inch) sticks. Chop the remainder coarsely. Cut half the ginger into matchsticks, and finely chop the rest. Blanch the carrot sticks in boiling water for 1 minute, refresh them immediately in cold water and drain.

Preheat the oven to 130°C (250°F or Mark ½). Put 15 g (½ oz) of the butter in a heavy frying pan and sauté the whole shallots over medium heat until they begin to soften and turn golden-brown — 4 to 5 minutes. Pour in the 2 tablespoons of wine and the honey, increase the heat and boil, stirring frequently, until the liquid reduces to a syrupy glaze. Place the shallots in a roasting pan in the oven.

Cut the lamb across the grain into 16 medallions. Season them with the salt and freshly ground pepper.

Melt the remaining butter in a heavy frying pan over low heat. Sauté the ginger matchsticks for 2 to 3 seconds, add the carrot sticks and sauté them for 10 seconds, then add the rhubarb sticks and sauté all the ingredients for a further 10 seconds, stirring all the time. Remove the sticks with a slotted spoon, transfer them to a plate, cover them and keep warm.

Increase the heat to high and brown the medallions for 1 to 2 minutes on each side. Put them in the roasting pan in the oven with the glazed shallots.

To finish making the sauce, pour off any fat from the frying pan. Put the pan over high heat, pour in the red wine and bring it to the boil, stirring to dislodge any meat deposits. Add the chopped shallots together with the chopped ginger, carrots and rhubarb. Boil until only half the liquid remains, then add the stock and the honey and continue boiling until the liquid is reduced by half again. Strain the sauce through a fine sieve into a clean saucepan. Add the carrot and rhubarb sticks and the ginger matchsticks and heat through.

Place four medallions on each of four warmed plates, pour the sauce round them and garnish with the spring onions. Serve with the glazed shallots.

SUGGESTED ACCOMPANIMENT: *rice noodles.*

Lamb and Broccoli Stir-Fry

Serves 4
Working (and total) time: about 25 minutes

Calories **245**
Protein **22g**
Cholesterol **50mg**
Total fat **8g**
Saturated fat **3g**
Sodium **270mg**

350 g	lean lamb (from the loin), cut into thin strips	12 oz
4 tsp	safflower oil	4 tsp
20 g	fermented black beans, soaked in water for 5 minutes	¾ oz
½ tsp	sesame oil	½ tsp
1	onion, halved lengthwise, cut into strips	1
2	garlic cloves, finely chopped	2
2.5 cm	piece fresh ginger root, finely chopped	1 inch
175 g	broccoli, blanched, stalks peeled and julienned, flowers divided into florets	6 oz
2	sticks celery, chopped	2
1	sweet red pepper, seeded, deribbed and thinly sliced	1
1 tsp	low-sodium soy sauce or shoyu	1 tsp
200 g	fresh water chestnuts, peeled and boiled for 3 minutes, or canned water chestnuts, drained	7 oz
3 tbsp	medium sherry	3 tbsp

Heat 1 teaspoon of the safflower oil in a wok or a large heavy frying pan and stir-fry half of the lamb over a medium heat, tossing and stirring until it is browned — about 2 minutes. Remove the lamb from the wok and keep it warm. Heat another teaspoon of the oil in the wok, stir-fry the remaining meat and add it to the first batch.

Drain the black beans and mash them in a small bowl with the sesame oil to make a coarse paste. Set aside. Put the remaining safflower oil into the wok or frying pan, add the onion, chopped garlic and ginger and stir-fry for 1 minute. Add the broccoli, celery, red pepper and soy sauce and stir-fry for a further 2 minutes. Add the water chestnuts, black bean paste and sherry, and return the lamb to the wok. Stir-fry over medium heat for a further 2 minutes, so that all the ingredients are coated with the sauce and heated through. Serve immediately.

SUGGESTED ACCOMPANIMENT: *plain boiled rice.*

Lamb Medallions on Courgette Pancakes

Serves 4
Working (and total) time: about 30 minutes

Calories **235**
Protein **26g**
Cholesterol **70mg**
Total fat **9g**
Saturated fat **4g**
Sodium **295mg**

1 kg	loin, boned and trimmed of fat, eye only (page 134)	2 ¼ lb
3 tbsp	cut chives or finely chopped spring onions, for garnish	3 tbsp
Courgette pancakes		
350 g	courgettes, grated	12 oz
1	carrot, grated	1
1	egg white	1
3 tbsp	freshly grated Parmesan cheese	3 tbsp
2 tbsp	wholemeal flour	2 tbsp
2	garlic cloves, finely chopped	2
¼ tsp	salt	¼ tsp
	freshly ground black pepper	
1 tsp	safflower oil	1 tsp

Cut the eye of loin into eight slices. With a meat bat or the flat of a heavy knife, pound each slice between plastic film or greaseproof paper, as shown on page 24, to a thickness of about 5 mm (¼ inch). Set the medallions aside.

Combine all the pancake ingredients except the oil in a bowl and mix them well.

Heat a large, non-stick frying pan over medium heat. Add the oil and spread it over the bottom with a paper towel. Drop four 2 tablespoon mounds of the pancake mixture into the pan, allowing ample room between them. With a spatula, spread out each mound to form a pancake about 7.5 cm (3 inches) in diameter. Cook the pancakes until they are lightly browned — about 3 minutes on each side. Transfer the pancakes to a baking sheet and keep them warm in a very low oven. Cook four more pancakes in the same way.

Increase the heat under the pan to high. Add the medallions to the pan and cook them until they are browned — about 2 minutes on each side.

Put two courgette pancakes on each of four plates; top each pancake with a lamb medallion. Sprinkle the medallions with the cut chives or chopped spring onions, and serve at once.

SUGGESTED ACCOMPANIMENT: *tomato wedges with basil.*

EDITOR'S NOTE: *Only the eye of the loin is used here; reserve the fillet for another recipe where lean meat is called for.*

Peppered Steaks with Bean Sprout Salad

Serves 4
Working (and total) time: about 40 minutes

Calories **260**
Protein **28g**
Cholesterol **80mg**
Total fat **12g**
Saturated fat **4g**
Sodium **330mg**

4	boned steaks (about 140 g/4 ½ oz each), cut from the fillet end of the leg, trimmed of fat	4
2 tsp	black peppercorns	2 tsp
¼ tsp	salt	¼ tsp
1 tbsp	virgin olive oil	1 tbsp
3 tbsp	brandy	3 tbsp
30 cl	unsalted chicken stock (recipe, page 137)	½ pint
1 tbsp	cornflour	1 tbsp
	celery leaves, for garnish	
	Bean sprout salad	
2 tsp	Dijon mustard	2 tsp
½	lemon, juice only	½
3 tbsp	thick Greek yogurt	3 tbsp
1 tbsp	chopped parsley	1 tbsp
¼ tsp	salt	¼ tsp
	freshly ground black pepper	
175 g	bean sprouts, rinsed and drained well	6 oz
10 cm	piece cucumber, julienned	4 inch
3	sticks celery, chopped	3
1	small sweet red pepper, seeded, deribbed and thinly sliced	1

First prepare the salad. Put the mustard, lemon juice, yogurt and parsley into a salad bowl, season with the salt and some pepper, and mix well together. Add the bean sprouts, cucumber, celery and red pepper. Stir all the salad ingredients thoroughly, then cover the bowl and refrigerate while cooking the steaks.

Crush the peppercorns coarsely using a mortar and pestle. Cut each steak into two neat pieces, then coat them on both sides with the crushed peppercorns and season with the salt.

Heat the olive oil over medium heat in a large, heavy frying pan. Add the steaks and cook them for 3 to 4 minutes on each side for rare to medium meat. Using a slotted spoon, transfer the steaks to a hot serving dish. Cover them and keep them hot.

Skim off any fat from the frying pan. Pour in the brandy, heat it for a few seconds, then ignite it using a taper. As soon as the flame subsides, add the stock and bring the liquid to the boil, stirring and scraping the sediment from the bottom of the pan into the sauce. In a small bowl, blend the cornflour with 1 tablespoon of cold water, then stir it into the sauce. Bring the sauce to the boil, reduce the heat and simmer for 2 to 3 minutes, stirring frequently, until the sauce thickens.

Strain the sauce over and round the peppered steaks. Garnish them with the celery leaves and serve immediately, accompanied by the bean sprout salad.

SUGGESTED ACCOMPANIMENT: *small baked potatoes*.

Loin and Liver Cassis

Serves 4
Working time: about 30 minutes
Total time: about 40 minutes

Calories **175**
Protein **18g**
Cholesterol **105mg**
Total fat **8g**
Saturated fat **3g**
Sodium **35mg**

300 g	lean lamb (from the loin) trimmed of fat, thinly sliced and flattened to about 3 mm (⅛ inch) thick (page 24)	10 oz
60 g	lamb's liver, very thinly sliced	2 oz
12	shallots	12
7 g	unsalted butter	¼ oz
2 tbsp	plus 1 tsp crème de cassis	2 tbsp
1 ½ tsp	blackcurrant or red wine vinegar	1 ½ tsp
¾ tsp	salt	¾ tsp
15 cl	unsalted chicken stock (recipe, page 137)	¼ pint
2 tsp	plain flour	2 tsp
	freshly ground black pepper	

Place the shallots in a small, heavy-bottomed, non-reactive saucepan with the butter, the teaspoon of *crème de cassis*, ½ teaspoon of the vinegar, ¼ teaspoon of the salt and 3 tablespoons of water. Cover tightly, bring to the boil and simmer until the shallots are tender — about 25 minutes. Remove the lid, increase the heat and boil off the residual liquid to glaze the shallots, shaking the pan occasionally to prevent them from burning. Set the shallots aside and keep them warm.

Meanwhile, pour the stock and the remaining *crème de cassis* into a separate non-reactive saucepan. Boil it rapidly until the liquid has reduced by about one half — 5 to 10 minutes. Set the reduced stock aside.

Sift the flour with some pepper and toss the liver in the seasoned flour until it is evenly coated. Brush a large, heavy frying pan lightly with oil, place it over very high heat and sear the slices of loin for 20 to 30 seconds on each side. Transfer them to a heated serving dish, sprinkle them with pepper and keep them warm. Reduce the heat to low, brush the pan with a little more oil and cook the floured slices of liver for 20 to 30 seconds, stirring constantly. Remove the liver and set it aside.

Increase the heat under the pan and add the remaining teaspoon of vinegar. Allow it to bubble for a few seconds, then add the reduced stock and the remaining ½ teaspoon of salt. Bring to the boil, return the liver to the pan and simmer for a further 30 seconds before spooning the sauce and liver over the slices of loin. Serve with the glazed shallots.

SUGGESTED ACCOMPANIMENTS: *steamed mange-tout; mashed potato sprinkled with chopped parsley.*

Kasha-Coated Lamb with Parsley-Garlic Sauce

Serves 4
Working (and total) time: about 20 minutes

Calories **410**
Protein **35g**
Cholesterol **85mg**
Total fat **14g**
Saturated fat **5g**
Sodium **75mg**

4	lamb slices (about 125 g /4 oz each), cut from the fillet end of the leg, trimmed of fat and flattened to about 5 mm (¼ inch) thick (page 24)	4
1	egg white	1
1 tbsp	fresh lemon juice	1 tbsp
200 g	toasted buckwheat groats (kasha)	7 oz
¼ tsp	salt	¼ tsp
	freshly ground black pepper	
1 tbsp	virgin olive oil	1 tbsp
½ tbsp	unsalted butter	½ tbsp
1	shallot, finely chopped	1
1	garlic clove, finely chopped	1
60 g	parsley, chopped	2 oz
1	large ripe tomato, skinned, seeded and puréed in a food processor or blender	1

In a shallow bowl, whisk together the egg white and lemon juice. Spread the buckwheat groats on a plate. Sprinkle the lamb slices with the salt and some pepper. Dip a slice in the egg white mixture, then dredge it in the buckwheat groats, coating both sides. Repeat the process to coat the remaining slices of lamb.

Heat the oil and butter in a large, heavy or non-stick frying pan over high heat. Add the coated lamb slices and cook them until they are lightly browned on one side — about 3 minutes. Turn the slices and cook them for 2 minutes more to brown the second side. Transfer the slices to a warmed platter.

Add the chopped shallot, garlic and parsley to the pan and cook them for 1 minute. Stir in the puréed tomato and a generous grinding of black pepper. Cook the mixture for 1 minute more, then pour it over the lamb slices. Serve immediately.

SUGGESTED ACCOMPANIMENTS: *egg noodles; carrot purée.*

Lamb with Aubergine and Parmesan

Serves 4
Working time: about 40 minutes
Total time: about 1 hour

Calories **450**		
Protein **34g**		
Cholesterol **80mg**		
Total fat **10g**		
Saturated fat **4g**		
Sodium **235mg**		

500 g	lean lamb (from the leg or loin), trimmed of fat and cut into 1 cm (¼ inch) pieces	1 lb
250 g	pasta shells	8 oz
1 tsp	virgin olive oil	1 tsp
250 g	pearl onions, blanched in boiling water for 2 minutes and peeled	8 oz
250 g	small mushrooms, wiped clean	8 oz
350 g	aubergine, cut into 1 cm (½ inch) cubes	12 oz
1 tsp	fresh thyme, or ½ tsp dried thyme	1 tsp
	freshly ground black pepper	
15 g	Parmesan cheese, shaved with a vegetable peeler or grated	½ oz

Add the pasta to 3 litres (5 pints) of boiling water with 1½ teaspoons of salt. Start testing the pasta for done-ness after 6 minutes and cook it until it is *al dente*. Drain the pasta, rinse it under cold running water to prevent the shells from sticking together and set it aside while you cook the meat and vegetables.

Heat a large, non-stick sauté pan over high heat. Add the pieces of lamb and sauté them until they are browned on all sides — about 3 minutes. Reduce the heat to medium and cook the lamb for 3 minutes more. Remove the meat from the pan and set it aside.

Add the olive oil and onions to the sauté pan. Cover the pan and cook the onions, stirring occasionally, until they are browned — about 15 minutes. Add the mush-rooms and aubergine cubes, then increase the heat to high, and sauté the vegetables until all of them are browned and the mushrooms and aubergine are soft — 6 to 8 minutes.

Return the lamb to the pan; add the pasta, the thyme and a generous grinding of pepper. Sauté the mixture until the pasta is heated through — about 3 minutes. Spoon the mixture into a warmed serving dish and top it with the cheese. Serve immediately.

SUGGESTED ACCOMPANIMENT: *curly endive salad.*

Lamb Paprika

Serves 4
Working time: about 25 minutes
Total time: about 6 hours and 25 minutes
(includes marinating)

Calories **245**
Protein **30g**
Cholesterol **85mg**
Total fat **11g**
Saturated fat **5g**
Sodium **350mg**

500 g	lean lamb (from the fillet end of the leg), trimmed of fat and cut into thin strips	1 lb
1 tbsp	paprika	1 tbsp
¼ tsp	freshly ground black pepper	¼ tsp
½ tsp	salt	½ tsp
350 g	kale, washed, stemmed and chopped	12 oz
2 tsp	caraway seeds	2 tsp
15 g	polyunsaturated margarine	½ oz
1	garlic clove, crushed	1
3	shallots, thinly sliced	3
2	bay leaves	2
3	tomatoes, skinned and chopped	3
3 tbsp	medium-dry sherry	3 tbsp
2 tbsp	soured cream	2 tbsp

Put the lamb in a bowl with the paprika, the pepper and half of the salt, and stir until the meat is evenly coated. Cover the bowl and leave it in a cool place to marinate for at least 6 hours or overnight. Stir the meat once during this period.

Pour enough water into a large saucepan to fill it about 2.5 cm (1 inch) deep. Place a vegetable steamer in the pan and bring the water to the boil. Put the chopped kale in the steamer and sprinkle it with the remaining salt and the caraway seeds. Cover the saucepan and cook until the kale is just tender and bright green — 5 to 6 minutes.

Meanwhile, melt the margarine in a large, heavy frying pan. Stir in the garlic, shallots and bay leaves and cook them over medium heat until the shallots are softened — 1 to 2 minutes. Increase the heat to high and sauté the lamb, stirring occasionally, until it has changed colour all over — 2 to 3 minutes. Stir in the tomatoes and sherry. Bring the mixture to the boil and cook it for 2 minutes.

Spoon the kale into a hot serving dish, cover it and keep it warm. Transfer the lamb and its sauce to a second hot dish, stir in the soured cream and serve immediately, accompanied by the kale.

SUGGESTED ACCOMPANIMENT: *Melba toast.*

Stir-Fried Vegetables with Shredded Lamb

Serves 4
Working (and total) time: about 40 minutes

Calories **255**
Protein **21g**
Cholesterol **50mg**
Total fat **13g**
Saturated fat **3g**
Sodium **265mg**

350 g	lean lamb (from the loin), cut into thin strips	12 oz
4 tbsp	sake or dry sherry	4 tbsp
2 tbsp	low-sodium soy sauce or shoyu	2 tbsp
1 tsp	cornflour	1 tsp
2 tbsp	safflower oil	2 tbsp
1 tbsp	finely chopped fresh ginger root	1 tbsp
1	onion, peeled and sliced	1
175 g	baby sweetcorn, halved lengthwise if large	6 oz
1	sweet red pepper, seeded, deribbed and thinly sliced	1
175 g	cucumber, halved lengthwise, seeded and sliced	6 oz
175 g	small mange-tout, stems and strings removed	6 oz

Mix together the sake, soy sauce and cornflour in a small bowl and set the mixture aside.

Heat the oil in a wok or large, heavy sauté pan until it is hot but not smoking. Add the chopped ginger and onion slices, and stir-fry for 1 minute over high heat, then add the baby sweetcorn and continue to stir-fry for 1 more minute.

Add the strips of lamb a few at a time, stirring constantly until they are completely sealed and lightly coloured, then add the pepper and cucumber and stir-fry for a further minute.

Lastly, add the mange-tout and stir-fry for 1 minute.

Pour the sake mixture over the meat and vegetables in the wok and bring it to the boil, stirring until the liquid thickens. Serve immediately.

SUGGESTED ACCOMPANIMENT: *rice or noodles.*

Loin and Liver in Yellow Bean Sauce

Serves 4
Working time: about 20 minutes
Total time: about 30 minutes

Calories **235**
Protein **22g**
Cholesterol **265mg**
Total fat **13g**
Saturated fat **3g**
Sodium **425mg**

175 g	lean lamb (from the loin), trimmed of fat and cut into thin strips	6 oz
175 g	lamb's liver, cut into thin strips	6 oz
2 tsp	light low-sodium soy sauce	2 tsp
2 tsp	Chinese rice wine or dry sherry	2 tsp
1 tsp	sesame oil	1 tsp
1½ tsp	cornflour	1½ tsp
200 g	spring onions	7 oz
2 cm	piece fresh ginger root	¾ inch
1	garlic clove	1
2 tsp	safflower oil	2 tsp
½	fresh red chili pepper, seeded and thinly sliced (caution, page 83)	½
	nori seaweed, shredded, for garnish	

Yellow bean sauce		
3 tbsp	yellow bean sauce	3 tbsp
½ tsp	sugar	½ tsp
1 tsp	dark low-sodium soy sauce or shoyu	1 tsp
2 tsp	Chinese rice wine or dry sherry	2 tsp

Put the loin and liver strips into separate bowls. Blend together the light soy sauce, rice wine, sesame oil and cornflour and divide this marinade between the two bowls. Stir well to coat the meat thoroughly. Leave to marinate for 15 minutes. Mix together the ingredients for the yellow bean sauce and set the sauce aside.

Cut the spring onions into 6 cm (2½ inch) lengths. Cut the white sections in half lengthwise; keep the white and the green parts separate. Bruise the ginger and garlic with the side of a heavy knife.

Heat a wok over medium heat and add the safflower oil. Drop in the ginger and garlic and let them sizzle until they turn light brown. Using the tip of a spatula, rub the garlic and ginger all round the wok, then remove and discard them.

Increase the heat to high. Stir-fry the loin, followed by the liver, the white parts of the spring onions and the yellow bean sauce, by constantly tossing and stirring each ingredient for about 15 seconds before adding the next. If the food seems about to stick and burn, lift the wok off the heat for a few seconds. Add the chili and stir-fry for another 10 seconds, then stir in the green parts of the spring onions.

Serve the mixture immediately, garnished with a little shredded nori.

SUGGESTED ACCOMPANIMENT: *egg noodles.*

a wide, heavy frying pan until it is very hot but not smoking. Brown the meat for 30 seconds on each side, then remove it from the pan and season it with ½ teaspoon of the salt and some black pepper. Keep it warm while preparing the salad.

Skim off any fat from the pan juices, then add the cucumber bâtonnets and cook gently over medium heat until they begin to soften — about 1½ minutes. Transfer them to a large bowl and add the endive.

To make the dressing, strain the reserved marinade into the frying pan and boil it over high heat until only 3 tablespoons of liquid remain. Remove the pan from the heat, stir in the *crème fraîche* and cook over low heat for 1 minute. Again remove the pan from the heat, and stir in the yogurt, the sugar and the remaining dill, chervil and salt. Pour the warm dressing over the endive and cucumber in the bowl, toss the salad and arrange it on four individual plates. Place the strips of lamb on top and serve immediately.

SUGGESTED ACCOMPANIMENT: *granary rolls.*

Warm Herbed Salad

Serves 4
Working time: about 30 minutes
Total time: about 3 hours and 30 minutes
(includes marinating)

Calories **260**		
Protein **31g**		
Cholesterol **90mg**		
Total fat **14g**		
Saturated fat **6g**		
Sodium **380mg**		

4	lamb slices (about 125 g/4 oz each), cut from the fillet end of the leg, trimmed of fat and flattened to about 3 mm (¼ inch) thick (box, right)	4
12.5 cl	dry white wine	4 fl oz
1 tbsp	chopped fresh tarragon	1 tbsp
4 tsp	chopped fresh dill	4 tsp
4 tsp	chopped fresh chervil	4 tsp
1 tbsp	safflower oil	1 tbsp
¾ tsp	salt	¾ tsp
	freshly ground black pepper	
100 g	cucumber, cut into bâtonnets	3½ oz
200 g	Batavian endive, washed and dried, trimmed and shredded	7 oz
2 tbsp	crème fraîche	2 tbsp
3 tbsp	thick Greek yogurt	3 tbsp
¼ tsp	sugar	¼ tsp

Cut each slice of meat into five strips. Place the meat in a shallow dish with the wine, the tarragon and 3 teaspoons each of the dill and chervil. Leave the meat to marinate for 3 to 4 hours, turning it half way through.

Remove the meat from the marinade and dry it well on paper towels; reserve the marinade. Heat the oil in

Flattening Escalopes

POUNDING THE MEAT. Trim off all visible fat and membrane from the meat. Place the meat between two sheets of plastic film. Using a wooden bat or the flat of a large, heavy knife, pound the meat gently to the thickness called for in the recipe.

Lamb Stroganoff

Serves 4
Working (and total) time: about 25 minutes

Calories **230**		
Protein **29g**		

500 g	lean lamb (from the loin), trimmed of fat and cut into thin strips	1 lb
1 tbsp	virgin olive oil	1 tbsp
1	onion, finely chopped	1
250 g	mushrooms, thinly sliced	8 oz
4 tbsp	thick Greek yogurt	4 tbsp
1 tsp	Dijon mustard	1 tsp
¼ tsp	salt	¼ tsp
	freshly ground black pepper	
1 tbsp	chopped parsley	1 tbsp
1 tbsp	finely cut chives	1 tbsp

Calories **230**
Protein **29g**
Cholesterol **80mg**
Total fat **12g**
Saturated fat **5g**
Sodium **175mg**

Heat the oil in a large, heavy frying pan over medium heat. Add the onion and cook it gently until soft but not brown — 6 to 8 minutes. Transfer the onion to a plate.

Add half of the lamb strips to the frying pan and cook them over high heat until they are lightly browned — 1 to 2 minutes — then transfer them to the plate with the onion. Brown the remaining lamb strips, then return the first batch of lamb and the onion to the pan.

Add the mushrooms and cook over medium heat until they soften — 4 to 5 minutes. Away from the heat, stir the yogurt and mustard into the mixture, then heat it through gently for 3 to 4 minutes. Season with the salt and some black pepper.

Transfer the stroganoff to a serving dish. Sprinkle it with the parsley and chives and serve immediately.

SUGGESTED ACCOMPANIMENT: *mashed potato nests filled with puréed peas.*

Escalopes with Mustard and Tarragon

Serves 4
Working (and total) time: about 20 minutes

Calories **255**		
Protein **30g**		
Cholesterol **75mg**		
Total fat **12g**		
Saturated fat **5g**		
Sodium **140mg**		

4	lamb slices (about 125 g/4 oz each), from the fillet end of the leg, trimmed of fat, flattened to about 3 mm (⅛ inch) thick (page 24)	4
50 g	dry wholemeal breadcrumbs	1¾ oz
1 tbsp	chopped fresh tarragon, or 1 tsp dried tarragon	1 tbsp
2 tbsp	chopped parsley	2 tbsp
½	lemon, grated rind only	½
	freshly ground black pepper	
2 tbsp	Dijon mustard	2 tbsp
1 tbsp	virgin olive oil	1 tbsp
4	lemon wedges, for garnish	4

Mix together the breadcrumbs, tarragon, parsley, lemon rind and some pepper. Sprinkle the mixture on to a large sheet of greaseproof paper. Cut the lamb slices in half. Using a brush, lightly coat one side of each slice with the mustard. Set a slice, mustard side down, on the crumb mixture, then turn it to coat the other side. Repeat with the remaining slices.

Heat half of the oil in a large, heavy frying pan over medium-high heat and sauté four of the escalopes until they are golden-brown — 1½ to 2 minutes each side. Keep them warm while you cook the remaining four escalopes in the rest of the oil. Garnish each portion with a lemon wedge and serve immediately.

SUGGESTED ACCOMPANIMENT: *a salad of young spinach, bulb fennel and tomatoes.*

Lamb and Barley Salad

Serves 4
Working time: about 20 minutes
Total time: about 2 hours (includes chilling)

Calories			
265			

Calories **265**
Protein **21g**
Cholesterol **50mg**
Total fat **10g**
Saturated fat **4g**
Sodium **275mg**

350 g	lean lamb (from the leg or loin), trimmed of fat and cut into 1 cm (½ inch) cubes	12 oz
100 g	pearl barley	3 ½ oz
1 ½ tbsp	finely chopped fresh oregano, or ½ tbsp dried oregano	1 ½ tbsp
1 ½ tbsp	virgin olive oil	1 ½ tbsp
¼ tsp	salt	¼ tsp
	freshly ground black pepper	
3 tbsp	red wine vinegar	3 tbsp
1	large ripe tomato, seeded and chopped	1
1	stick celery, chopped	1
90 g	red onion, chopped	3 oz
	lettuce leaves, for garnish	

Put the barley, half of the oregano and ¾ litre (1¼ pints) of water into a saucepan. Bring the water to the boil, then reduce the heat to maintain a steady simmer. Cover the pan and cook the barley until it is tender — about 50 minutes. Drain the barley, transfer it to a bowl, and stir in ½ tablespoon of the oil.

Heat the remaining oil in a heavy frying pan set over high heat. Add the lamb cubes and sprinkle them with the salt and some freshly ground pepper. Sauté the cubes, stirring frequently, until they are lightly browned — about 2 minutes. Pour in the vinegar and cook the mixture for 30 seconds longer.

Transfer the contents of the pan to the bowl with the barley. Add the tomato, celery, onion, the remaining oregano and a generous grinding of pepper. Toss the salad well and chill it for at least 1 hour.

Just before serving, arrange the lettuce leaves on a plate or platter and mound the salad on top.

SUGGESTED ACCOMPANIMENT: *orange and watercress salad.*

Marinated Cutlets with Caper and Parsley Sauce

Serves 6
Working time: about 30 minutes
Total time: about 2 hours and 30 minutes
(includes marinating)

Calories **255**
Protein **27g**
Cholesterol **85mg**
Total fat **15g**
Saturated fat **3g**
Sodium **170mg**

12	best end of neck cutlets (about 90 g/3 oz each), trimmed of fat	12
1 tsp	virgin olive oil	1 tsp
1	garlic clove, finely chopped	1
1 tbsp	chopped parsley	1 tbsp
1 tsp	chopped fresh marjoram, or ¼ tsp dried marjoram	1 tsp
1 tsp	chopped fresh thyme, or ¼ tsp dried thyme	1 tsp
¼ tsp	salt	¼ tsp
½ tsp	freshly ground black pepper	½ tsp
	Caper and parsley sauce	
1 tsp	cornflour	1 tsp
8 cl	skimmed milk	3 fl oz
75 g	crème fraîche	2½ oz
4	pickled onions, finely chopped	4
2 tbsp	chopped parsley	2 tbsp
1 tbsp	finely chopped capers	1 tbsp
	freshly ground black pepper	

Using a sharp knife, scrape the ends of the rib bones free of any flesh or skin. Place the cutlets in a large shallow dish. Combine the olive oil, garlic, parsley, marjoram, thyme, salt and freshly ground pepper, and brush this mixture over both sides of the cutlets. Cover the dish and leave the cutlets to marinate in the refrigerator for 2 to 4 hours.

Preheat the grill to high while you make the sauce. Mix the cornflour with 1 tablespoon of the milk. Bring the remaining milk nearly to the boil in a small saucepan, add the cornflour paste and cook over low heat, stirring, until the milk thickens — 2 to 3 minutes. Stir in the crème fraîche, pickled onions, parsley, capers and some pepper. Heat the sauce through, remove it from the heat and keep it warm while cooking the cutlets.

Cook the cutlets for 3 to 4 minutes on each side for rare to medium meat and serve them with the sauce.

SUGGESTED ACCOMPANIMENTS: *oven-baked potato chips; braised leeks.*

Cutlets with Pernod

Serves 4
Working time: about 25 minutes
Total time: about 2 hours and 30 minutes
(includes marinating)

Calories **260**
Protein **29g**
Cholesterol **75mg**
Total fat **13g**
Saturated fat **6g**
Sodium **280mg**

8	best end of neck cutlets (about 90 g/3 oz each), trimmed of fat	8
2	limes, finely grated rind and juice	2
4 tbsp	plain low-fat yogurt	4 tbsp
2 tbsp	Pernod or other anise-flavoured spirit	2 tbsp
1 tbsp	chopped fresh thyme, or 1 tsp dried thyme	1 tbsp
2	garlic cloves, crushed	2
1 tsp	muscovado sugar	1 tsp
	freshly ground black pepper	
1 tsp	cornflour	1 tsp
½ tsp	salt	½ tsp
	lime wedges, for garnish	
	thyme sprigs, for garnish (optional)	

Put the lime rind and juice in a shallow dish with the yogurt, Pernod, thyme, crushed garlic, sugar and some freshly ground pepper. Whisk together with a fork, then place the lamb cutlets in the dish and turn them to coat them evenly. Cover the dish and leave the cutlets to marinate in the refrigerator for at least 2 hours, or preferably overnight.

Preheat the grill to high. Lift the cutlets out of the marinade, reserving the marinade, and grill them for 3 to 4 minutes on each side for rare to medium meat. While the cutlets are grilling, put the cornflour into a

saucepan, blend in the marinade and add the salt. Bring the sauce to the boil and simmer for 3 minutes, stirring constantly. Arrange the cutlets on a warm serving dish and garnish with the lime wedges and thyme sprigs, if you are using them. Pass the sauce separately.

SUGGESTED ACCOMPANIMENT: *steamed baby carrots.*

Sichuan Peppercorn Lamb

Serves 4
Working time: about 30 minutes
Total time: about 45 minutes

Calories **290**
Protein **32g**
Cholesterol **80mg**
Total fat **14g**
Saturated fat **5g**
Sodium **135mg**

4	loin chops (about 150 g/5 oz each), trimmed of fat (page 135)	4
2 tsp	Sichuan peppercorns	2 tsp
1 tbsp	shoyu or low-sodium soy sauce	1 tbsp
1 tbsp	dry sherry	1 tbsp
125 g	French beans, topped and tailed, cut in half	4 oz
½ tbsp	safflower oil	½ tbsp
1 tbsp	finely chopped spring onions	1 tbsp
1	large carrot, peeled and julienned	1
1	sweet red pepper, seeded, deribbed and julienned	1
	green ends of spring onions, sliced diagonally, for garnish	

Heat a heavy-bottomed pan over medium heat and toast the peppercorns by stirring them until their aroma increases — about 30 seconds. Grind them to a fine powder with a mortar and pestle, then mix 1 teaspoon of ground peppercorns together with the shoyu and sherry in a shallow dish. Place the chops in the dish, turn them to coat them and leave to marinate for 20 minutes; turn them once during this time.

Meanwhile, parboil the French beans in boiling water for 3 minutes. Drain and rinse them under cold running water. Drain again and set them aside. Preheat the grill to high.

Remove the chops from the dish and discard the marinade. Dust the chops with the remaining crushed peppercorns, and pin the flap of lean meat to the eye of each chop with a cocktail stick. Grill the chops for 4 to 6 minutes on each side for rare to medium meat.

While the chops are cooking, stir-fry the vegetables. In a wok or heavy frying pan, heat the oil until it is hot but not smoking. Add the chopped spring onions and fry them for 30 seconds, stirring constantly, then add the julienned carrot and pepper, and the beans. Stir-fry all the vegetables for 2 minutes, then serve them immediately alongside the grilled chops. Garnish the chops with the spring onion slices.

SUGGESTED ACCOMPANIMENT: *egg noodles.*

Noisettes with Julienned Vegetables

Serves 4
Working time: about 45 minutes
Total time: about 1 hour

Calories **265**
Protein **38g**
Cholesterol **100mg**
Total fat **10g**
Saturated fat **5g**
Sodium **260mg**

1	rack of lamb (about 1 kg/2 ¼ lb), boned and trimmed of fat (page 136, Steps 1 to 4)	1
¼ tsp	salt	¼ tsp
	freshly ground black pepper	
1 tsp	finely chopped fresh oregano, or ¼ tsp dried oregano	1 tsp
2	large carrots, trimmed and julienned	2
3	sticks celery, trimmed and julienned	3
1	parsnip, peeled and julienned	1
2	leeks, trimmed, washed and julienned	2
1 tbsp	chopped parsley	1 tbsp

Season the boned side of the meat with the salt, a little pepper and the oregano. Following the technique shown in Step 5 on page 136, roll the lamb into a cylinder, with the eye of the meat in the centre, and tie the roll at eight equally spaced intervals. Cut the roll into slices midway between each tie. Place the noisettes on the grill rack and set them aside.

Preheat the grill to high. Pour enough water into a saucepan to fill it 2.5 cm (1 inch) deep. Set a vegetable steamer in the pan and bring the water to the boil. Put the julienned carrots, celery and parsnip into the steamer, cover tightly, and steam for about 5 minutes;

add the leeks and continue to steam for a further 3 minutes, until the vegetables are tender but still crisp.

Meanwhile, grill the noisettes for 3 to 5 minutes on each side for rare to medium meat. When the vegetables are cooked, toss them in the parsley.

Arrange the noisettes on a warm serving dish and surround them with the julienned vegetables.

SUGGESTED ACCOMPANIMENTS: *cranberry sauce; puréed potatoes.*

Noisettes in a Fig Sauce

Serves 4
Working and total time: about 35 minutes

Calories **205**	8	loin chops (about 100 g/3½ oz each) trimmed of fat, boned and tied into noisettes	8
Protein **27g**			
Cholesterol **80mg**			
Total fat **7g**	6	dried figs, finely chopped	6
Saturated fat **3g**	2 tbsp	balsamic vinegar, or 1½ tbsp red wine vinegar mixed with ½ tsp honey	2 tbsp
Sodium **270mg**			
	2 tbsp	Madeira	2 tbsp
	2 tsp	Worcester sauce	2 tsp
	20 cl	unsalted chicken stock (recipe, page 137)	7 fl oz
	½ tsp	salt	½ tsp
		freshly ground black pepper	
	4	fresh figs, sliced	4

Preheat the grill to high while you make the sauce. Put the dried figs, vinegar, Madeira and Worcester sauce in a small saucepan and simmer until the liquid reduces to a thick syrup — 4 to 5 minutes. Add the chicken stock and bring the mixture to the boil; reduce the heat and simmer uncovered for 2 minutes. Remove the saucepan from the heat and press the mixture through a sieve to make a smooth sauce. Return the sauce to the pan and keep it warm, uncovered, over low heat while you cook the noisettes.

Season the noisettes with the salt and some freshly ground pepper and grill them for 2 to 4 minutes on each side for rare to medium meat. Serve immediately with the sauce and sliced fresh figs.

SUGGESTED ACCOMPANIMENT: *steamed broccoli.*

Noisettes with Glazed Potatoes and Gooseberry Purée

Serves 6
Working time: about 45 minutes
Total time: about 1 hour

Calories **280**
Protein **31g**
Cholesterol **75mg**
Total fat **11g**
Saturated fat **5g**
Sodium **195mg**

2	racks of lamb (about 600g/1 ¼ lb each), trimmed of fat, boned, tied and cut into 12 noisettes (page 136)	2
2 tsp	virgin olive oil	2 tsp
	freshly ground black pepper	
7 g	unsalted butter	¼ oz
2	shallots, finely chopped	2
15 cl	unsalted chicken stock (recipe, page 137)	¼ pint
⅛ tsp	salt	⅛ tsp
400 g	tiny new potatoes, scrubbed	14 oz
	fresh chervil, for garnish	
Minted gooseberry purée		
500 g	fresh gooseberries, topped and tailed, or frozen gooseberries, thawed	1 lb
2	mint sprigs plus six leaves	2
1 tsp	light brown sugar	1 tsp
¼ tsp	salt	¼ tsp

Brush the noisettes with the olive oil and rub them all over with freshly ground pepper. Arrange them on a grill pan and set them aside.

To make the purée, place the gooseberries in a heavy-bottomed, non-reactive saucepan, together with the sprigs of mint, the sugar and 1 tablespoon of water. Cover and cook gently until the gooseberries are soft — 15 to 30 minutes. Remove the mint sprigs and purée the gooseberries in a blender with the fresh mint leaves and the salt. Pass the purée through a nylon sieve; set it aside and keep it warm.

Melt the butter in a heavy-bottomed saucepan and gently cook the shallots, covered, until they are soft — about 5 minutes. Add the stock and salt, bring it to the boil, then add the potatoes and cook them, partly-covered, until they are tender — 20 to 25 minutes. Meanwhile, preheat the grill to high.

Remove the lid from the pan and boil the stock rapidly until no liquid remains and the potatoes are glossy — about 3 minutes. Shake the pan regularly during this process to prevent the potatoes and shallots from singeing. Keep warm until ready to serve.

Grill the noisettes for 3 to 4 minutes on each side for rare to medium meat. Arrange them on a warm serving platter with the glazed potatoes and garnish with chervil. Serve the purée separately.

SUGGESTED ACCOMPANIMENT: *French beans or peas.*

Boning a Butterfly Chop

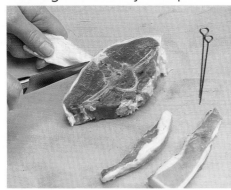

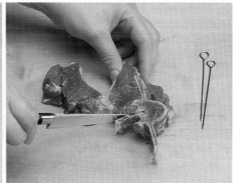

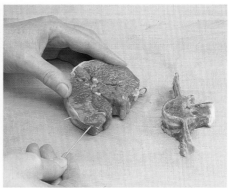

1 *TRIMMING OFF THE FAT. Using a small, sharp knife, cut off the two fatty side flaps where they join the chop. Peel the skin and fat from the back of the chop, leaving the connective tissue and fat above the bone intact (above).*

2 *REMOVING THE BONE. Insert the knife point into the base of the chop and carefully run it round the contours of the bone to free the meat. Take care not to cut through the connective tissue.*

3 *SECURING THE CHOP. Bring the sides of the chop together to form a neat circular shape. Secure the chop with two skewers.*

Crusted Butterfly Chops with Peppercorn Sauce

Serves 4
Working time: about 40 minutes
Total time: about 1 hour

Calories **215**
Protein **32g**
Cholesterol **75mg**
Total fat **14g**
Saturated fat **7g**
Sodium **270mg**

4	double loin butterfly chops (about 175 g/6 oz each), trimmed of fat, boned and secured with skewers (opposite, below)	4
4	slices white bread	4
1	garlic clove, peeled	1
1	shallot, finely chopped	1
175 g	button mushrooms, wiped and finely chopped	6 oz
1 tsp	grated lemon rind	1 tsp
1 tsp	chopped fresh thyme, or ¼ tsp dried thyme	1 tsp
1 tbsp	chopped parsley	1 tbsp
1½ tsp	fresh green peppercorns, or green peppercorns in brine, rinsed	1½ tsp
15 cl	unsalted chicken or veal stock (recipes, page 137)	¼ pint
⅛ tsp	salt	⅛ tsp
2 tbsp	fresh white or brown breadcrumbs	2 tbsp
15 g	Lancashire cheese, or other white crumbly cheese, grated	½ oz
2 tbsp	thick Greek yogurt or soured cream	2 tbsp

Preheat the oven to 180°C (350°F or Mark 4). Cut out four circles from the bread, each slightly larger in diameter than the butterfly chops. Bake them in the oven until they are golden-brown — 20 to 25 minutes — then rub one side of each with the garlic clove and keep them warm. Preheat the grill to high.

While the croûtes are baking, brush a heavy, non-stick frying pan with oil, place it over high heat and stir-fry the chopped shallot for 2 minutes. Add the mushrooms and soften them over a moderate heat for 4 minutes, then increase the heat and cook them rapidly for a minute or two to reduce excess moisture. Remove the pan from the heat, stir in the lemon rind, thyme and parsley and set the pan aside.

Grill the butterfly steaks for 4 to 6 minutes each side for rare to medium meat. Meanwhile, heat a small, shallow pan and dry-fry the peppercorns for 30 seconds. Pour in the stock and boil it rapidly until it has reduced by half — about 4 minutes. Remove the chops from the grill and set them aside. Skim the fat from the juices in the grill pan, then pour the juices into the reduced stock. Season the sauce with the salt, and set it over low heat to keep warm.

Spoon the mushroom mixture neatly on to the chops. Mix the breadcrumbs with the grated cheese, then sprinkle the breadcrumb mixture over the mushrooms. Return the chops to the grill until the cheese turns golden-brown. Remove the skewers. Set each crusted chop on top of a croûte.

Remove the sauce from the heat and stir in the yogurt or cream. Serve the sauce with the chops.

SUGGESTED ACCOMPANIMENT: *steamed asparagus.*

Sweet and Spicy Grilled Lamb

Serves 4
Working time: about 1 hour
Total time: about 2 hours (includes marinating)

Calories **310**
Protein **23g**
Cholesterol **70mg**
Total fat **8g**
Saturated fat **3g**
Sodium **205mg**

1 kg	loin, boned and trimmed of fat, eye only (page 134)	2¼ lb
	freshly ground black pepper	
¼ tsp	ground allspice	¼ tsp
¼ tsp	ground cloves	¼ tsp
2 tbsp	fresh lemon juice	2 tbsp

2 tbsp	light brown sugar	2 tbsp
	Cherry ketchup	
225 g	sweet cherries, stoned	7½ oz
4 tbsp	light brown sugar	4 tbsp
¼ tsp	salt	¼ tsp
6 tbsp	cider vinegar	6 tbsp
7.5 cm	strip of lemon rind	3 inch
½ tsp	ground ginger	½ tsp
2	cinnamon sticks	2
⅛ tsp	cayenne pepper	⅛ tsp

To make the ketchup, combine the cherries, brown sugar, salt, vinegar, lemon rind, ginger, cinnamon sticks and cayenne pepper in a heavy-bottomed saucepan. Bring the mixture to a simmer and cook it until it has thickened — about 15 minutes. Discard the cinnamon sticks and pour the mixture into a food processor or blender. Purée the mixture, then strain it into a small bowl and allow it to cool.

To prepare a marinade for the meat, mix a generous grinding of pepper with the allspice, cloves, lemon juice and brown sugar in a small bowl. Put the eye of loin in a shallow dish and pour the marinade over it, rubbing the spices into the meat. Let the lamb marinate at room temperature for 1 hour, turning it every 15 minutes.

If you plan to barbecue the meat, light the charcoal about 30 minutes before cooking time; to grill, preheat the grill for about 10 minutes. Remove the lamb from the marinade and cook it for 5 to 7 minutes on each side, brushing it occasionally with any marinade remaining in the dish. Let the lamb rest for about 5 minutes before slicing it. Serve the ketchup separately.

SUGGESTED ACCOMPANIMENT: *steamed cauliflower.*

EDITOR'S NOTE: *Only the eye of the loin is used here; reserve the fillet for another recipe where lean meat is called for.*

Steaks with Grated Courgettes and a Tomato Coulis

Serves 4
Working time: about 25 minutes
Total time: about 45 minutes

Calories **280**			
Protein **31g**	4	boneless steaks (about 140 g/4½ oz each), cut from the fillet end of the leg and trimmed of fat, or butterfly steaks, boned (page 32)	4
Cholesterol **75mg**			
Total fat **13g**	400 g	courgettes	14 oz
Saturated fat **5g**	1 tsp	salt	1 tsp
Sodium **395mg**	1 tbsp	virgin olive oil	1 tbsp
	2 tbsp	chopped fresh marjoram, or 2 tsp dried marjoram	2 tbsp

	freshly ground black pepper	
	ribbon-thin lengthwise slices of courgette, for garnish (optional)	
	Tomato coulis	
1 tsp	virgin olive oil	1 tsp
2	garlic cloves, finely chopped	2
750 g	ripe tomatoes, skinned, seeded and finely chopped, or 400 g (14 oz) canned tomatoes, chopped	1½ lb
1 tbsp	chopped fresh oregano, or 1 tsp dried oregano	1 tbsp
1 tsp	chopped fresh marjoram, or ¼ tsp dried marjoram	1 tsp
	freshly ground black pepper	
8 cl	medium-dry white wine	3 fl oz

Trim the courgettes and grate them coarsely, then transfer them to a sieve set over a bowl. Stir in half a teaspoon of the salt and allow the courgettes to stand for 30 minutes.

Meanwhile, brush the steaks with the oil, rub them with half of the marjoram and sprinkle them with black pepper. Using cocktail sticks or skewers, pin the steaks into neat rounds and set them aside.

To make the tomato coulis, heat the oil in a heavy-bottomed saucepan. Add the garlic and cook it for 1 minute over medium-high heat. Add the tomatoes, oregano, marjoram and some pepper. Cook until the tomatoes are reduced to a purée — about 10 minutes. Add the wine, heat the coulis through and keep it warm. Preheat the grill to medium.

Season the steaks with the remaining salt and grill them for 5 to 6 minutes each side for rare to medium meat. While they are grilling, squeeze the courgettes dry with your hands and stir-fry them with the remaining marjoram in a non-stick saucepan over medium-low heat until they soften — about 3 minutes.

When the steaks are cooked, remove the cocktail sticks or skewers. Spread the courgette mixture evenly on top of each steak. Pour a little of the tomato coulis on to each of four warmed plates, and arrange the steaks on top. Garnish with the strips of courgette, if you are using them, and serve immediately.

SUGGESTED ACCOMPANIMENT: *wholemeal bread.*

Grilled Lamb with Chutney Glaze and Mint

Serves 10
Working time: about 30 minutes
Total time: about 1 hour and 15 minutes

Calories **200**
Protein **23g**
Cholesterol **75mg**
Total fat **8g**
Saturated fat **3g**
Sodium **135mg**

2.5 kg	leg of lamb, trimmed of fat and boned	5 lb
1 tbsp	safflower oil	1 tbsp
1/4 tsp	salt	1/4 tsp
	freshly ground black pepper	
4 tbsp	chopped mint	4 tbsp
	mint sprigs, for garnish	
Chutney glaze		
1/4 litre	unsalted brown or chicken stock (recipes, page 137)	8 fl oz
4 tbsp	mango chutney	4 tbsp
1/2 tbsp	dry mustard	1/2 tbsp
1 tbsp	cider vinegar	1 tbsp
1/2 tbsp	cornflour, mixed with 1 tbsp water	1/2 tbsp

First, prepare the lamb. Spread the boned leg of lamb flat on a work surface with the cut side of the meat facing upwards. Cut out the membranes and tendons and discard them. Starting from the centre of the meat, slice horizontally into the flesh at one side of the leg, making sure that you do not cut completely through the meat. Open out the resulting flap, then slice into the opposite side of the leg and open it out in a similar manner. The meat should be no more than 5 cm (2 inches) thick.

If you plan to barbecue the lamb, light the charcoal about 30 minutes before cooking time; to grill the meat, preheat the grill for 10 minutes.

To make the chutney glaze, combine the stock and the mango chutney in a small saucepan and bring the mixture to a simmer over medium heat. Stir the mustard and the cider vinegar into the cornflour paste and then whisk this mixture into the simmering stock and chutney. Cook the glaze, stirring continuously, until it thickens — about 1 minute. Remove the pan from the heat and set the glaze aside.

With your fingers, rub both sides of the lamb with the safflower oil. Grill the lamb, turning it every 5 minutes, until it is well browned on both sides — about 20 minutes in all. Sprinkle the salt and some freshly ground black pepper on the lamb and brush it with some of the chutney glaze. Continue cooking the lamb, turning and basting it frequently with the glaze, for about another 10 minutes. Pour the remaining chutney glaze into a small serving bowl.

Transfer the lamb to a cutting board and sprinkle it with the chopped mint. Allow the meat to stand for 10 minutes before carving it into slices. Arrange the slices of lamb on a warm serving platter and serve accompanied by the remaining chutney glaze and garnished with mint sprigs.

SUGGESTED ACCOMPANIMENT: *tomato and burghul salad.*

Leg of Lamb in
Spiced Apple Sauce

Serves 12
Working time: about 45 minutes
Total time: about 2 hours and 25 minutes (includes marinating)

2	cloves	2
¼ tsp	ground cinnamon	¼ tsp
⅛ tsp	ground allspice	⅛ tsp

To make the apple sauce, cook the apples gently in a heavy-bottomed saucepan with 1 tablespoon of water, until they are soft and fluffy. Drain off any excess liquid then purée the apples by pressing them through a nylon sieve. Return the purée to the saucepan, add the sugar, cloves, ground cinnamon and allspice, and cook the sauce over low heat, stirring occasionally, until the mixture has reduced to about 12.5 cl (4 fl oz) and has a thick spreading consistency. Remove the cloves and set the sauce aside to cool a little while you prepare the meat.

Spread the boned leg of lamb flat on a work surface with the cut side of the meat facing upwards. Cut out the membranes and tendons and discard them. Starting from the centre of the meat, slice horizontally into the flesh at one side of the leg, making sure that you do not cut completely through the meat. Open out the resulting flap, then slice into the opposite side of the leg and open it out in a similar manner. The meat should be no more than 5 cm (2 inches) thick.

Put the apple sauce into a large bowl and mix in the vinegar, onion, garlic, sage, salt, pepper and oil. Put the butterflied lamb into the bowl and spread the apple sauce mixture thickly all over it. Leave the lamb in the bowl to marinate at room temperature for about 1 hour, turning it after 30 minutes.

If you plan to barbecue the lamb, light the charcoal about 30 minutes before cooking time; to grill it preheat the grill for 10 minutes. Remove the lamb from the marinade, holding it over the bowl to allow any excess marinade to drip off. Reserve the marinade.

Cook the lamb for 12 minutes on each side for medium-rare meat. Baste the lamb from time to time with the reserved marinade.

Leave the lamb to rest for about 15 minutes, then carve it into slices and serve.

Calories **225**
Protein **30g**
Cholesterol **80mg**
Total fat **9g**
Saturated fat **4g**
Sodium **135mg**

2.5 kg	leg of lamb, trimmed of fat and boned	5 lb
4 tbsp	cider vinegar	4 tbsp
1	onion, finely chopped	1
2	garlic cloves, finely chopped	2
1 tbsp	finely chopped fresh sage, or 1 ½ tsp dried sage	1 tbsp
½ tsp	salt	½ tsp
1 tbsp	freshly ground black pepper	1 tbsp
1 tbsp	safflower oil	1 tbsp
Spiced apple sauce		
300 g	cooking apples, peeled, cored and sliced	10 oz
30 g	sugar	1 oz

SUGGESTED ACCOMPANIMENT: *steamed courgettes; baked sweet potatoes.*

Flambéed Kebabs

Serves 6
Working time: about 50 minutes
Total time: about 3 hours and 50 minutes
(includes marinating)

Calories **255**
Protein **30g**
Cholesterol **75mg**
Total fat **11g**
Saturated fat **4g**
Sodium **100mg**

750 g	eye and fillet of loin, trimmed of fat and cut into 24 cubes	1 ½ lb
1	large courgette, thickly sliced	1
½	sweet green pepper, seeded and cut into 6 by 2.5 cm (2 ½ by 1 inch) strips	½
½	sweet red pepper, seeded and cut into 6 by 2.5 cm (2 ½ by 1 inch) strips	½
1	large onion, cut into 12 wedges	1
2	oranges, rind and pith removed, halved and cut into 1 cm (½ inch) slices	2
1	firm ripe mango, peeled and cut into six pieces	1
1 tbsp	virgin olive oil	1 tbsp
4 tbsp	brandy	4 tbsp
Orange and honey marinade		
1	orange, finely grated rind and strained juice only	1
3 tbsp	clear honey	3 tbsp
1	onion, finely grated	1
4	garlic cloves, crushed	4
1 tbsp	tomato paste	1 tbsp
1 tbsp	virgin olive oil	1 tbsp
1 tbsp	paprika	1 tbsp
½ tsp	salt	½ tsp
¼ tsp	cayenne pepper	¼ tsp

Put all of the marinade ingredients into a large mixing bowl and stir them well together. Add the cubes of lamb and stir until they are thoroughly coated with the marinade. Cover the bowl and allow the lamb to marinate at room temperature for 3 to 4 hours, turning it from time to time.

When you are ready to assemble the kebabs, blanch the courgette and peppers in boiling water for 2 to 3 minutes to soften them slightly. Transfer the vegetables to a colander and refresh them under cold running water. Drain well.

Preheat the grill to its highest setting. Thread the marinated lamb and pieces of courgette, pepper, onion, orange and mango alternately on six kebab skewers. Place the skewers on the grill rack and sprinkle them with the olive oil. Grill the kebabs for 10 to 15 minutes, carefully turning the skewers three or four times to ensure that they cook evenly. At the end of this time the lamb should be cooked, yet still slightly pink in the centre.

When the kebabs are ready, place them on a warmed dish. Put the brandy into a small shallow sauté pan and warm it over low heat for about 10 seconds. Standing well back, ignite the brandy in the pan with a taper and pour it, flaming, over the kebabs. Arrange the kebabs on a serving platter.

SUGGESTED ACCOMPANIMENTS: *saffron rice; cucumber and chili pepper salad.*

Lamb Tikka

IN THIS VERSION OF THE TRADITIONAL INDIAN TIKKA, CHUNKS
OF PINEAPPLE CREATE A REFRESHING CONTRAST TO THE
HIGHLY SPICED CUBED MEAT.

Serves 4
Working time: about 30 minutes
Total time: about 5 hours (includes marinating)

Calories **255**
Protein **32g**
Cholesterol **75mg**
Total fat **9g**
Saturated fat **4g**
Sodium **100mg**

500 g	lean lamb (from the loin or fillet end of leg), trimmed of fat and cut into 4 cm (1½ inch) cubes	1 lb
2.5 cm	piece fresh ginger root, peeled and coarsely chopped	1 inch
2	garlic cloves, coarsely chopped	2
2	green chili peppers, seeded and coarsely chopped (caution, page 83)	2
2 tsp	cumin seeds	2 tsp
1 tsp	ground turmeric	1 tsp
½ tsp	ground fenugreek	½ tsp
12	mint leaves	12
15 cl	plain low-fat yogurt	¼ pint
1 tbsp	fresh lime juice	1 tbsp
2	star anise pods	2
350 g	fresh pineapple, cut into chunks	12 oz

Put the meat in a bowl. In a blender or food processor, purée the ginger, garlic, chilies, cumin, turmeric, fenugreek and mint leaves. Add the yogurt and lime juice and blend to mix. Pour the purée over the meat, add the star anise and mix well to coat the meat thoroughly. Leave the lamb to marinate in a cool place for 4 to 6 hours, stirring occasionally.

Preheat the grill to hot. Thread the cubes of meat and pineapple alternately on to four metal kebab skewers; reserve the marinade. Place the kebabs on a grill rack and grill until the lamb is cooked but still slightly pink in the centre — 10 to 15 minutes. Turn the skewers frequently and baste the meat with the reserved marinade while grilling.

SUGGESTED ACCOMPANIMENTS: *brown rice; cucumber, mint and onion salad.*

Kebabs with Olive-Mint Sauce

Serves 4
Working time: about 25 minutes
Total time: about 40 minutes

Calories **240**
Protein **24g**
Cholesterol **75mg**
Total fat **12g**
Saturated fat **3g**
Sodium **295mg**

600 g	lean lamb (from the loin or fillet end of leg), trimmed of fat and cut into 16 cubes	1 ¼ lb
30 g	mint, chopped	1 oz
6	oil-cured black olives, stoned and finely chopped	6
1 tbsp	virgin olive oil	1 tbsp
½ tsp	ground allspice	½ tsp
	freshly ground black pepper	
2	onions, each cut into six wedges	2
½	sweet green pepper, seeded, deribbed and cut into eight pieces	½
½	red apple, cored and cut into eight pieces	½
¼ litre	unsalted brown or chicken stock (recipes, page 137)	8 fl oz
⅛ tsp	salt	⅛ tsp

If you plan to barbecue the lamb, light the charcoal about 30 minutes before cooking time; to grill, preheat the grill for 10 minutes.

Put the lamb cubes into a bowl with 3 tablespoons of the mint, half of the olives, ½ tablespoon of the oil, ¼ teaspoon of the allspice and a generous grinding of pepper. Stir the lamb cubes to coat them evenly with the marinade, then set the bowl aside at room temperature while you prepare the other ingredients.

Gently toss together the onions, green pepper, apple, 3 tablespoons of the remaining mint, the remaining olive oil and allspice and some black pepper in another bowl, and set it aside.

Pour the stock into a small saucepan over medium heat, then stir in the remaining olives, the remaining mint and the salt. Cook the sauce until only about 6 tablespoons remain — about 10 minutes. Remove the pan from the heat and set it aside.

Thread the lamb cubes and the vegetable and apple chunks on to four skewers. Grill the kebabs for 3 to 4 minutes on each side for medium meat. Transfer them to a platter. Reheat the sauce, pour it over the kebabs and serve immediately.

SUGGESTED ACCOMPANIMENT: *lentil and onion salad.*

Lamb Sausages on Skewers

Serves 4
Working time: about 30 minutes
Total time: about 1 hour and 10 minutes

Calories **245**
Protein **26g**
Cholesterol **75mg**
Total fat **11g**
Saturated fat **4g**
Sodium **320mg**

600 g	lean lamb (from the leg or loin), trimmed of fat and minced (page 43)	1¼ lb
1	large ripe tomato, seeded and chopped	1
¼ tsp	salt	¼ tsp
	freshly ground black pepper	
1 tsp	sugar	1 tsp
1 tbsp	red wine vinegar	1 tbsp
3 tbsp	chopped parsley	3 tbsp
1 tbsp	chopped fresh oregano, or 1 tsp dried oregano	1 tbsp
1	egg white	1
1 tbsp	virgin olive oil	1 tbsp
30 g	dry breadcrumbs	1 oz
2	spring onions, trimmed and thinly sliced	2
½ tsp	capers, rinsed	½ tsp
12.5 cl	plain low-fat yogurt	4 fl oz

Put the tomato, half of the salt, some pepper, the sugar and the vinegar into a heavy frying pan set over medium heat. Cook the mixture, stirring frequently, until only about 4 tablespoons remain — about 20 minutes. Transfer the mixture to a bowl and let it cool to room temperature.

In a large bowl, combine the minced lamb with 2 tablespoons of the parsley, the oregano, egg white, half of the oil, the breadcrumbs, half of the spring onions, the remaining salt and some pepper. Stir the cooled tomato mixture into the lamb mixture and refrigerate the bowl until the contents are thoroughly chilled — about 30 minutes.

If you plan to barbecue the sausages, light the charcoal about 30 minutes before cooking time; to grill, preheat the grill for 10 minutes.

Divide the lamb mixture into four portions and form each one into a sausage shape about 10 cm (4 inches) long. Thread each sausage on to a skewer, keeping the meat pressed firmly in place.

Pour the remaining oil on to a large, flat plate. Lightly coat the sausages by rolling them in the oil. Grill or barbecue the sausages, turning the skewers every now and then, until the meat is lightly browned — 8 to 10 minutes.

Meanwhile, finely chop the remaining parsley with the remaining spring onions and the capers. Transfer the chopped parsley mixture to a small bowl and whisk in the yogurt and some pepper. Serve the sausages immediately, passing the sauce separately.

SUGGESTED ACCOMPANIMENT: *couscous tossed with cinnamon and grated carrots.*

Kofta with Onion Sauce

COMMON IN INDIAN AND MIDDLE EASTERN COOKING, KOFTA
CONSISTS OF MINCED MEAT AND SEASONINGS ROLLED INTO
SAUSAGE SHAPES OR BALLS.

Serves 4
Working time: about 30 minutes
Total time: about 40 minutes

Calories **260**
Protein **27g**
Cholesterol **80mg**
Total fat **14g**
Saturated fat **5g**
Sodium **195mg**

500 g	lean lamb (from the leg or loin), trimmed of fat and minced (opposite page)	1 lb
1	onion, finely chopped	1
60 g	pitted olives, finely chopped	2 oz
2 tbsp	chopped fresh coriander	2 tbsp
1 tbsp	Worcester sauce	1 tbsp
¼ tsp	salt	¼ tsp
	freshly ground black pepper	
30 g	caul (optional)	1 oz
Onion sauce		
15 g	polyunsaturated margarine	½ oz
1	red onion, finely chopped	1
1 tsp	cumin seeds	1 tsp
2 tbsp	raspberry or cider vinegar	2 tbsp
1 tbsp	cornflour	1 tbsp
30 cl	unsalted brown stock (recipe, page 137)	½ pint
⅛ tsp	salt	⅛ tsp
	freshly ground black pepper	

First, make the onion sauce. Melt the margarine in a sauté pan or heavy frying pan. Add the onion and cumin seeds, and cook them over medium heat until the onions are soft — about 4 minutes. Add the vinegar and continue cooking until the liquid reduces to a thick syrup. Mix the cornflour to a paste with 2 tablespoons of the stock. Add the remaining stock to the pan and bring it to the boil. Add the cornflour paste and stir until the sauce thickens — 2 to 3 minutes. Season the sauce with the salt and some black pepper; keep it warm while you prepare the kofta.

Combine the lamb, onion, olives, coriander, Worcester sauce, salt and some pepper in a bowl and mix thoroughly by hand. Shape the meat into 20 thick sausages, each about 4 cm (1½ inches) long. If you like, wrap eight of the sausages with pieces of caul. Carefully thread the sausages on to four long metal skewers, alternating caul-wrapped ones with plain.

Preheat the grill to high and cook the kofta for 10 minutes, turning them once. Serve the kofta hot with the onion sauce.

SUGGESTED ACCOMPANIMENT: *crisp mixed lettuce salad.*

EDITOR'S NOTE: *Caul, the weblike fatty membrane that surrounds a pig's stomach, gives the meat a distinctive flavour and helps moisten lean minced meat during grilling.*

Lamb and Mushroom Burgers

Serves 4
Working time: about 30 minutes
Total time: about 1 hour and 5 minutes

Calories **350**
Protein **36g**
Cholesterol **80mg**
Total fat **10g**
Saturated fat **5g**
Sodium **450mg**

500 g	lean lamb (from the leg or loin), trimmed of fat and minced (below)	1 lb
3 tbsp	fresh granary or wholemeal breadcrumbs	3 tbsp
2 tbsp	fresh orange juice	2 tbsp
¼ tsp	finely grated lemon rind	¼ tsp
1 tbsp	chopped parsley	1 tbsp
2 tsp	finely cut chives	2 tsp
⅛ tsp	dried marjoram	⅛ tsp
⅛ tsp	salt	⅛ tsp
	freshly ground black pepper	
125 g	button mushrooms, wiped and finely chopped	4 oz
4	granary baps, split in half	4
	carrot ribbons, for garnish	
	finely chopped celery, for garnish	
	shredded cabbage, for garnish	
	flat-leaf parsley, for garnish	

Mustard sauce

1 tbsp	grainy mustard	1 tbsp
4 tbsp	fromage frais	4 tbsp
1 tbsp	finely cut chives	1 tbsp
	freshly ground black pepper	

Put the lamb, breadcrumbs, orange juice, lemon rind, parsley, chives, marjoram, salt and some pepper in a bowl and mix them thoroughly by hand. Set the bowl aside. Heat a heavy non-stick frying pan, brush it with oil, add the mushrooms and sauté them over high heat for 3 minutes, stirring them constantly. Allow the mushrooms to cool, then add them to the meat mixture. Shape the mixture into four burgers, each about 10 cm (4 inches) in diameter. Cover and refrigerate them for 30 minutes.

Meanwhile, combine the ingredients for the mustard sauce in a mixing bowl. Set the sauce aside.

Preheat the grill to hot, and cook the burgers for about 4 minutes on each side for medium meat. Toast the baps on the cut sides. Place each burger on the bottom half of a bap, garnish with the carrot, celery, cabbage and parsley, spoon on a portion of the mustard sauce and top with the other half of the bap.

SUGGESTED ACCOMPANIMENT: *oven-baked chips.*

Mincing by Hand

1 CUBING THE MEAT. Trim off all traces of fat and membrane from the meat and cut it into uniform slices. Place the slices on top of one another and cut through to make evenly sized strips. Cut the strips of lean meat into fairly small cubes (above).

2 MINCING THE MEAT. Spread the cubed meat out evenly on a chopping board and chop it with a matched pair of sharp, heavy knives. With a loose-wristed action, work the knives alternately and rhythmically, as if beating a drum (above). From time to time, use one of the knife blades to flip and turn the chopped mass back into the centre: this helps achieve a consistent texture. Continue chopping until the meat is minced as coarsely or finely as the recipe dictates.

Leg of Lamb with Pomegranate Sauce

Serves 8
Working time: about 30 minutes
Total time: about 1 hour and 30 minutes

Calories **250**
Protein **30g**
Cholesterol **90mg**
Total fat **8g**
Saturated fat **4g**
Sodium **130mg**

2.25 kg	leg of lamb, trimmed of fat	4½ lb
1 tbsp	fresh thyme	1 tbsp
1	pomegranate	1
1	lime, finely grated rind and juice only	1
1½ tbsp	redcurrant jelly	1½ tbsp
	finely grated lime rind, for garnish	
	watercress, for garnish	
Pomegranate sauce		
3	pomegranates	3
4 tbsp	redcurrant jelly	4 tbsp
1 tbsp	caster sugar	1 tbsp
2	limes, julienned rind and juice only	2
1½ tbsp	cornflour	1½ tbsp
8 cl	rosé wine	3 fl oz

Preheat the oven to 200°C (400°F or Mark 6).

Make four or five incisions into the flesh of the lamb and fill them with the thyme. Place the leg of lamb in a roasting pan.

Cut open the pomegranate and scoop out the seeds. Reserve one third of the seeds for garnish. Using a wooden spoon, press all the juice from the remaining seeds through a nylon sieve into a bowl. Stir the lime rind and juice into the pomegranate juice, then pour half of the combined juices over the lamb, coating the entire surface of the meat.

Place the joint in the oven and roast it, basting frequently, for 1 to 1¼ hours for rare to medium meat. Half way through the cooking time, pour the remaining lime and pomegranate juices over the lamb.

Remove the lamb from the oven, transfer it to a warm platter and allow it to rest in a warm place for about 20 minutes.

Meanwhile, make the pomegranate sauce. Cut open the pomegranates and scoop out the seeds into a nylon sieve set over a non-reactive saucepan. Press the juice from the seeds through the sieve. Stir in the redcurrant jelly, sugar and lime juice, then heat the mixture gently until the jelly and sugar have dissolved. Cook gently for 10 minutes. Blend the cornflour with the rosé wine and stir it into the sauce. Bring it to the boil and continue to cook, stirring, until the mixture thickens and clears — 2 to 3 minutes. Add the julienned lime rind, reduce the heat and simmer for a further 5 minutes, stirring frequently. Transfer the sauce to a warmed sauceboat.

Just before you are ready to carve, bring the redcurrant jelly to the boil and brush it over the meat. Sprinkle the meat with the reserved pomegranate seeds; garnish with the finely grated lime rind and watercress. Serve the sauce separately.

SUGGESTED ACCOMPANIMENTS: *boiled new potatoes; watercress salad.*

Roast Leg with Herbs and Garlic

Serves 8
Working time: about 30 minutes
Total time: about 3 hours (includes marinating)

Calories **260**	2.5 kg	leg of lamb, trimmed of fat	5 lb
Protein **8g**	3	garlic cloves	3
Cholesterol **100mg**	1 tsp	salt	1 tsp
Total fat **12g**	2 tbsp	chopped mixed fresh herbs (thyme, sage, rosemary, oregano), or 2 tsp mixed dried herbs	2 tbsp
Saturated fat **5g** Sodium **195mg**			
	1 tbsp	finely chopped parsley	1 tbsp
	1 tbsp	virgin olive oil	1 tbsp

Using a small pointed knife, make 10 to 12 deep, evenly spaced incisions into the flesh of the lamb.

With a pestle and mortar, crush together the garlic cloves and salt to make a creamy paste. Add the mixed herbs and the parsley. Using your fingers or a small teaspoon, fill each incision in the lamb with the herb and garlic paste. Rub the olive oil all over the leg, then place it in a roasting pan and set it aside in a cool place to marinate for 1 hour. Preheat the oven to 220°C (425°F or Mark 7).

Roast the leg for 15 minutes, then reduce the oven temperature to 190°C (375°F or Mark 5) and continue roasting for 50 minutes to 1 hour for rare to medium meat, basting the leg frequently with the pan juices. Transfer the leg to a serving dish, cover it loosely with foil and allow it to rest in a warm place for 20 to 30 minutes before carving.

SUGGESTED ACCOMPANIMENT: *haricot and French beans tossed in parsley.*

Leg of Lamb with Pear Mustard

Serves 10
Working time: about 1 hour
Total time: about 2 hours and 15 minutes

Calories **225**
Protein **24g**
Cholesterol **75mg**
Total fat **9g**
Saturated fat **3g**
Sodium **430mg**

2.5 kg	leg of lamb, trimmed of fat, the pelvic and thigh bones removed, the shank bone left in place	5 lb
½ tbsp	Dijon mustard	½ tbsp
1 tbsp	safflower oil	1 tbsp
¼ tsp	salt	¼ tsp
3	bunches spring onions, trimmed and cut into 2.5 cm (1 inch) lengths	3
Pear mustard		
½ tbsp	safflower oil	½ tbsp
750 g	pears, peeled, cored and coarsely chopped	1½ lb
¼ litre	unsalted brown or chicken stock (recipes, page 137)	8 fl oz
1½ tbsp	fresh lemon juice	1½ tbsp
1	shallot, finely chopped, or 1 spring onion, white part only, finely chopped	1
1	garlic clove, finely chopped	1
1¼ tsp	salt	1¼ tsp
	freshly ground black pepper	
1½ tbsp	Dijon mustard	1½ tbsp

To make the pear mustard, heat the oil in a heavy bottomed saucepan set over medium-high heat. Add the pears and cook them, stirring frequently, until the juice is syrupy and lightly browned — 15 to 20 minutes. Add the stock, lemon juice, shallot or spring onion, garlic, salt, some pepper and the mustard. Reduce the heat to medium and simmer the mixture, stirring occasionally, until only about 35 cl (12 fl oz) remain — 15 to 20 minutes. Transfer the pear mustard to a food processor or a blender and purée it until smooth.

Meanwhile, preheat the oven to 180°C (350°F or Mark 4) and prepare the leg of lamb for roasting. Rub the Dijon mustard over the exposed inner surface of the leg. Fold the meat over to enclose the mustard, then tie the leg securely with string. Heat the oil in a large, shallow fireproof casserole set over high heat. When the oil is hot, add the leg of lamb and brown it evenly on all sides — about 10 minutes. Sprinkle the lamb with the salt and transfer the casserole to the oven. Roast the lamb for 20 minutes.

Remove the lamb from the oven and coat it with about one third of the pear mustard, then roast it for 40 minutes more. Brush the lamb with about half of the remaining pear mustard. Increase the oven temperature to 240°C (475°F or Mark 9) and cook the lamb until the pear mustard is lightly browned in places — 10 to 15 minutes. Remove from the oven and let it rest in a warm place for 20 minutes.

Blanch the spring onion pieces in boiling water for 1 minute, then drain them and divide them among 10 warmed dinner plates. Slice the lamb and arrange the slices on the spring onions; spoon a little of the remaining pear mustard on top before serving.

SUGGESTED ACCOMPANIMENT: *a gratin of sliced turnips and sweet potatoes.*

Leg Roasted with Ginger

Serves 10
Working time: about 25 minutes
Total time: about 4 hours and 40 minutes
(includes marinating)

Calories **185**
Protein **24g**
Cholesterol **75g**
Total fat **7g**
Saturated fat **3g**
Sodium **170mg**

2.5 kg	leg of lamb, trimmed of fat	5 lb
3 tbsp	finely chopped fresh ginger root	3 tbsp
3	garlic cloves, finely chopped	3
2 tsp	low-sodium soy sauce or shoyu	2 tsp
¼ tsp	dark sesame oil	¼ tsp
1 tsp	rice vinegar or distilled white vinegar	1 tsp
6 tbsp	mirin or sweet sherry	6 tbsp
⅛ tsp	white pepper	⅛ tsp
Soy and sesame sauce		
1 tbsp	low-sodium soy sauce or shoyu	1 tbsp
2 tbsp	mirin or sweet sherry	2 tbsp
1 tsp	sesame seeds	1 tsp
2 tsp	rice vinegar or distilled white vinegar	2 tsp
1	spring onion, trimmed and thinly sliced	1
1	small carrot, sliced into thin rounds	1
2 tbsp	chopped fresh ginger root	2 tbsp
12.5 cl	unsalted brown or chicken stock (recipes, page 137)	4 fl oz

With a knife, lightly score the surface of the lamb in a crisscross pattern. Transfer the lamb to a shallow baking dish. Mix the ginger, garlic, soy sauce, sesame oil, vinegar, mirin or sherry and pepper in a small bowl. Pour this marinade over the lamb and refrigerate it for at least 3 hours, or as long as overnight. From time to time, baste the lamb with the marinade.

Towards the end of the marinating time, preheat the oven to 230°C (450°F or Mark 8). Transfer the lamb to a roasting pan, reserving the marinade, and roast for 10 minutes. Reduce the oven temperature to 180°C (350°F or Mark 4) and continue roasting the lamb for 1 hour for medium-rare meat. Baste the lamb from time to time with the reserved marinade during this period. Let the lamb rest in a warm place for 20 minutes before carving it.

While the lamb is resting, combine the sauce ingredients. Serve the sauce at room temperature with the sliced lamb.

SUGGESTED ACCOMPANIMENT: *a cold salad of Asian noodles.*

Garlic-Studded Lamb Shanks with Roasted Onions

Serves 4
Working time: about 20 minutes
Total time: about 2 hours

Calories **285**
Protein **31g**
Cholesterol **85mg**
Total fat **9g**
Saturated fat **3g**
Sodium **290mg**

4	lamb shanks (about 350 g/12 oz each), trimmed	4
6	garlic cloves, each cut lengthwise into four slices	6
½ tbsp	virgin olive oil	½ tbsp
1 tbsp	finely chopped fresh rosemary, or ½ tbsp dried rosemary	1 tbsp
	freshly ground black pepper	
¼ tsp	salt	¼ tsp
4	onions, unpeeled	4
6	carrots, cut into bâtonnets and blanched for 1 minute in boiling water	6

Preheat the oven to 180°C (350°F or Mark 4).

With the point of a knife, make an incision in the flesh of a shank; press a garlic slice deep into the opening. Repeat the process to insert six garlic slices into each shank. Rub the shanks with the oil, then sprinkle them with the rosemary and pepper. Put the shanks in a heavy roasting pan and roast them until they are very tender — 1 ½ to 2 hours.

After the lamb shanks have been roasting for 45 minutes, sprinkle them with the salt. Wrap the onions individually in aluminium foil and set them in the oven next to the roasting pan.

When the shanks are done, transfer them to a serving platter. Skim off the fat that has collected in the roasting pan, leaving any caramelized juices in the pan. Set the pan on the stove top over medium heat. Add the blanched carrots and cook them, stirring occasionally, for 2 minutes. Pour 4 tablespoons of water into the pan and bring the liquid to a simmer, scraping up the caramelized pan juices with a wooden spoon.

Transfer the carrots and the sauce to the platter. Unwrap the onions, cut off 1 cm (½ inch) from their tops and set them on the platter just before serving.

SUGGESTED ACCOMPANIMENTS: *steamed cabbage; Italian bread.*

EDITOR'S NOTE: *Shanks, the knuckle end of the hind leg or fore leg, are not always available and may have to be ordered from the butcher in advance. If unobtainable, use chump chops (about 175 g/6 oz each). Prepare them in the same way as the shanks, but cut the cooking time by half.*

Leg of Lamb Stuffed with Vegetables

Serves 10
Working time: about 40 minutes
Total time: about 2 hours

Calories **240**
Protein **25g**
Cholesterol **75mg**
Total fat **11g**
Saturated fat **4g**
Sodium **235mg**

2.5 kg	leg of lamb, trimmed of fat and boned	5 lb
2 tbsp	safflower oil	2 tbsp
1	large carrot, julienned	1
1	large courgette, julienned	1
1	large yellow squash, julienned	1
12.5 cl	dry sherry	4 fl oz
30 g	Parmesan cheese, freshly grated	1 oz
½ tsp	salt	½ tsp
	freshly ground black pepper	
1 tbsp	fresh thyme, or 2 tsp dried thyme	1 tbsp
¼ litre	unsalted brown or chicken stock (recipes, page 137)	8 fl oz
2 tbsp	finely chopped shallot or onion	2 tbsp
1½ tbsp	cornflour, mixed with 2 tbsp water	1½ tbsp

To prepare the stuffing, heat 1 tablespoon of the oil in a large, shallow fireproof casserole over medium heat. Add the carrot and sauté it, stirring often, for 2 minutes. Stir in the courgette and squash, and cook the vegetables until the carrot is barely tender — about 2 minutes more. Remove the casserole from the heat and pour in 2 tablespoons of the sherry. Add the Parmesan cheese and toss the stuffing to mix it well.

Preheat the oven to 170°C (325°F or Mark 3). Spread out the boned leg of lamb on a work surface and season it with half the salt, some pepper and half the thyme. Spread the stuffing over the leg of lamb and roll it up as you would a Swiss roll. Tie the leg of lamb with string to secure it.

Wipe out the casserole and heat the remaining oil in it over high heat. Add the lamb roll and brown it on all sides — 2 to 3 minutes altogether. Put the casserole into the oven and roast the lamb until it is tender — about 1 hour. Transfer the roast to a serving platter and set it aside to rest in a warm place.

Skim off the fat and set the casserole on the stove top over low heat. Add the stock, the remaining thyme, the shallot or onion and the remaining sherry to the casserole, then scrape the bottom with a wooden spoon to dissolve the caramelized roasting juices. Increase the heat to medium high and boil the liquid until about one third of it remains — 7 to 10 minutes. Reduce the heat to low and whisk in the cornflour mixture. Cook the sauce, stirring continuously, until it has thickened — about 1 minute. Season the sauce with the remaining salt and some pepper.

Cut the roast into slices. Pour the sauce into a warmed sauceboat and serve it separately.

SUGGESTED ACCOMPANIMENTS: *broccoli; mashed potatoes.*

Roast Shoulder with Rosemary

Serves 12
Working time: about 40 minutes
Total time: about 3 hours (includes marinating)

Calories **310**
Protein **20g**
Cholesterol **75mg**
Total fat **12g**
Saturated fat **5g**
Sodium **130mg**

2.5 kg	shoulder of lamb, trimmed of fat	5 lb
1 tbsp	virgin olive oil	1 tbsp
2 tsp	mixed dried herbs	2 tsp
½ tsp	salt	½ tsp
4	long rosemary sprigs	4
1 ½ tsp	plain flour	1 ½ tsp
60 cl	unsalted chicken or brown stock (recipes, page 137)	1 pint
	freshly ground black pepper	

Make four diagonal incisions with a sharp knife across the shoulder, almost down to the bone. Rub the olive oil, mixed herbs and salt all over the lamb, then insert the rosemary sprigs in the diagonal cuts. Place the shoulder in a roasting pan and set it aside in a cool place to marinate for 1 hour. Preheat the oven to 220°C (425°F or Mark 7).

Roast the shoulder for 15 minutes, then reduce the oven temperature to 190°C (375°F or Mark 5) and roast the meat for a further 45 minutes to 1 hour for rare to medium meat, basting frequently with the pan juices. Transfer the shoulder to a serving dish, cover it loosely with foil and set it aside to rest in a warm place while you make the gravy.

Tip the roasting pan slightly so that the juices run to one corner, then skim off any fat. Sprinkle the flour over the juices left in the pan and stir well with a wooden spoon until the juices and flour are smoothly blended. Gradually add the stock, stirring continuously. Place the pan over moderate heat and bring the gravy to the boil, stirring all the time until it thickens; season with some black pepper. Reduce the heat to low and simmer for 6 to 8 minutes, stirring occasionally. Strain the gravy through a sieve into a warmed gravy boat and serve it with the roast shoulder.

SUGGESTED ACCOMPANIMENTS: *steamed swede and parsnips; shredded spring greens.*

Shoulder Stuffed with Wild Rice and Spinach

Serves 12
Working time: about 1 hour
Total time: about 4 hours

Calories **225**
Protein **22g**
Cholesterol **75mg**
Total fat **13g**
Saturated fat **5g**
Sodium **140mg**

1.5 kg	shoulder of lamb, boned and trimmed of fat	3 lb
60 g	wild rice	2 oz
2 tsp	virgin olive oil	2 tsp
4	shallots, coarsely chopped	4
175 g	celeriac, grated	6 oz
175 g	fresh spinach, washed, stems removed	6 oz
½ tsp	finely grated nutmeg	½ tsp
¾ tsp	salt	¾ tsp
	freshly ground black pepper	
30 cl	unsalted chicken stock (recipe page 137)	½ pint
1 tsp	cornflour	1 tsp

To make the stuffing, wash the wild rice and put it into a large saucepan in twice its volume of water. Bring the water to the boil, cover the pan and simmer until the husks have split and the rice is soft — 50 minutes to 1 hour. Drain the rice and allow it to cool. Heat the oil in a frying pan, add the shallots and cook them over very low heat until they are soft but not brown. Add the celeriac and continue cooking until it begins to look transparent — about 3 minutes — then add the spinach and cook for about 1 minute, until it wilts. Blend this mixture very briefly in a food processor to make a rough-textured purée; do not over process. Mix the purée with the wild rice, and season with the nutmeg, ½ teaspoon of the salt and some black pepper.

Preheat the oven to 230°C (450°F or Mark 8). Stuff and tie the shoulder into a melon shape (page 52). Put ▶

the lamb in a roasting pan and season the outside with the remaining salt and some pepper. Roast the lamb in the oven until it is well browned — 10 to 15 minutes — then reduce the oven temperature to 200°C (400°F or Mark 6) and cook for a further 1¼ to 1½ hours for medium-rare to medium meat. Transfer the lamb to a carving board and allow it to rest in a warm place for 15 minutes.

While the meat is resting, make the gravy. Skim off any fat from the surface of the roasting juices and transfer the pan to the stove top. Add the stock and boil it over high heat, stirring to loosen any sediment from the bottom of the pan. Mix the cornflour with 1 tablespoon of water and add it to the pan, stirring constantly until the gravy thickens — 2 to 3 minutes. Season with black pepper. Cut off the string and carve the lamb into wedges. Serve the gravy separately.

SUGGESTED ACCOMPANIMENT: *steamed courgettes and mushrooms.*

Stuffing and Tying a Boned Shoulder

1 *STUFFING THE MEAT. Lay a boned shoulder of lamb, inner side uppermost, on the work surface. Open up the cavity left by the shoulder blade and fill it with stuffing (above). Fold two opposite sides of the shoulder over so that the stuffing is covered.*

2 *ENCLOSING THE STUFFING. Push a threaded trussing needle through the ends of the two flaps that were folded over in Step 1. Take the string out of the needle and tie the string, pulling the flaps tightly together. Fold over the other two sides to enclose the stuffing; stitch them (above) and tie them together.*

3 *FORMING A MELON SHAPE. Cut six pieces of string each about 60 cm (24 inches) long. Tie one length round the meat, pulling the string tight, then tie a second length across the first to section the meat into quarters. Continue tying the shoulder until it is divided into 12 segments and resembles a melon in shape.*

Roast Saddle of Lamb with Plum Sauce

Serves 12
Working time: about 1 hour
Total time: about 2 hours and 40 minutes

Calories **335**
Protein **28g**
Cholesterol **75mg**
Total fat **14g**
Saturated fat **6g**
Sodium **180mg**

4.5 kg	saddle of lamb	10 lb
1 tbsp	virgin olive oil	1 tbsp
2 tbsp	demerara sugar	2 tbsp
¾ tsp	salt	¾ tsp
	freshly ground black pepper	
750 g	large purple plums, halved and stoned	1½ lb
60 cl	red wine	1 pint
2.5 cm	piece cinnamon stick	1 inch
15 cl	unsalted chicken stock (recipe, page 137)	¼ pint
Fruit garnish		
3	dessert apples	3
60 g	caster sugar	2 oz
2 tbsp	fresh lemon juice	2 tbsp
6	large purple plums, halved, stoned and sliced	6

Preheat the oven to 220°C (425°F or Mark 7). Spread the saddle of lamb out flat on a cutting board and trim off the fatty strip, or apron, of flesh along each side; leave just enough to overlap slightly when tucked underneath the saddle. Carefully remove excess fat from the meat.

Rub the olive oil all over the meat, then sprinkle it with the sugar, ½ teaspoon of the salt and some black pepper. Tuck the side flaps neatly under the saddle and place it in a large roasting pan.

Roast the saddle for 20 minutes, then reduce the oven temperature to 180°C (350°F or Mark 4) and place the halved plums in the roasting pan, tucking them closely round the lamb. Pour half of the wine over the lamb and add the piece of cinnamon. Continue roasting for 1¼ to 1½ hours for rare to medium meat. Baste the meat frequently while it roasts; each time you baste, add some more of the wine until it is all used up.

Ten minutes before the lamb is cooked, begin to prepare the garnish. Peel and core the apples and cut them into 5 mm (¼ inch) thick rings. Put the caster sugar into a wide, shallow, non-reactive saucepan with the lemon juice and 15 cl (¼ pint) of cold water. Heat gently until the sugar dissolves. Cook the apple rings in the sugar syrup until they are soft but still firm — 3 to 5 minutes. Using a slotted spoon, transfer the apple rings to a plate. Cover the apples and keep them warm. Add the sliced plums to the syrup in the pan and cook them until they begin to soften — about 1 minute. Transfer the plums to the plate with the apple rings. Reduce the syrup by boiling rapidly until it thickens slightly — 2 to 3 minutes. Set it aside.

When the lamb is cooked, carefully transfer it to a large, hot serving platter. Cover it with foil and allow it to rest in a warm place for about 20 minutes.

Meanwhile, make the plum sauce. Set a nylon sieve over a non-reactive saucepan and pour the juices from the roasting pan into it. Using a wooden spoon, press the halved plums through the sieve into the saucepan. Stir the chicken stock into the plum mixture and season it with the remaining salt and some black pepper. Heat the sauce through, then pour it into a warmed sauce boat.

Garnish the roast lamb with the plums and apple rings, and brush the fruit slices with the syrup. Serve with the plum sauce.

SUGGESTED ACCOMPANIMENTS: *new potatoes; French beans.*

EDITOR'S NOTE: *The long saddle of lamb comprises the loin and chump.*

Rack of Lamb with a Spiced Parsley Crust

Serves 6
Working time: about 30 minutes
Total time: about 4 hours and 45 minutes
(includes marinating)

Calories **260**
Protein **30g**
Cholesterol **75mg**
Total fat **8g**
Saturated fat **4g**
Sodium **200mg**

2	750 g (1½ lb) racks of lamb, each with six cutlets, chine bones removed, bone trips shortened by 5 cm (2 inches), trimmed of fat and prepared for roasting (page 135)	2
1	small onion, finely chopped	1
2	garlic cloves, crushed	2
15 g	parsley, finely chopped	½ oz
¼ tsp	ground cumin	¼ tsp
¼ tsp	paprika	¼ tsp
½ tsp	salt	½ tsp
	freshly ground black pepper	
1 tsp	saffron threads, soaked in 1 tsp boiling water for 1 hour	1 tsp
15 cl	white wine	¼ pint
1 tsp	cornflour	1 tsp

In a small bowl, thoroughly mix together the onion, garlic, parsley, cumin, paprika, half the salt and some pepper. Stir in the saffron and its soaking liquid. Spread this mixture over the outer, fleshy side of the racks and leave them to marinate in a cool place, loosely covered, for 4 to 6 hours.

Preheat the oven to 220°C (425°F or Mark 7). Place the meat on a rack in a roasting pan, marinated side upwards. Roast for 25 minutes, then add the wine and 15 cl (¼ pint) of water to the roasting pan and return the meat to the oven until the crusts are turning dark round the edges — about 20 minutes. (The meat will still be slightly pink in the centre; cover the racks with foil and roast them for a further 15 minutes if you like your lamb more thoroughly cooked.)

When the meat is cooked, transfer it to a warmed plate. Skim off the fat from the cooking liquid, and boil the liquid rapidly to reduce it slightly. Mix the corn-flour with 1 tablespoon of water and stir it into the pan. Continue cooking over medium heat until the gravy thickens — 2 to 3 minutes. Season the gravy with the remaining salt and some black pepper, and pour it into a warmed gravy boat. Slice the racks into cutlets and serve them with the gravy.

SUGGESTED ACCOMPANIMENTS: *new potatoes; French beans.*

Guard of Honour

Serves 7
Working time: about 35 minutes
Total time: about 1 hour and 35 minutes

Calories **220** Protein **28g** Cholesterol **75mg** Total fat **9g** Saturated fat **3g** Sodium **125mg**			
	2	850 g (1 ¾ lb) racks of lamb, each with seven cutlets, chine bones removed, bone tips shortened by 5 cm (2 inches), trimmed of fat and prepared for roasting (page 135)	2
	1	garlic clove, halved	1
		freshly ground black pepper	
	1 tbsp	tahini	1 tbsp
	1 tbsp	Dijon mustard	1 tbsp
	1 tbsp	clear honey	1 tbsp
	1 tbsp	mustard seeds	1 tbsp
	1 ½ tbsp	sesame seeds	1 ½ tbsp
	1 tbsp	finely chopped fresh tarragon, or 1 tsp dried tarragon	1 tbsp

Red wine gravy

12.5 cl	red wine	4 fl oz
15 cl	unsalted chicken or brown stock (recipes, page 137), or water	¼ pint
1	sprig fresh tarragon, or ¼ tsp dried tarragon	1
½ tsp	clear honey	½ tsp
¼ tsp	salt	¼ tsp

Rub the garlic clove all over the flesh and bones, and season the meat generously with black pepper.

Mix together the tahini, mustard, honey, mustard seeds and sesame seeds. Combine 2 teaspoons of this paste with the chopped tarragon and spread the mixture over the concave inside of the racks.

Preheat the oven to 230°C (450°F or Mark 8). Assemble the guard by interlocking the exposed rib bone tips. Using string, tie the racks as shown on page 56. To prevent charring during cooking, cover the exposed bone tips with a single layer of aluminium foil, pressing the foil round the bones.

Spread the remaining tahini-mustard paste over the outside surface of the assembled guard. Place the meat in a roasting pan.

Roast the lamb for 50 minutes to 1 hour and 10 minutes for rare to medium meat. Transfer the guard to a warm platter, cut away the strings, and set it aside to rest in a warm place.

To make the gravy, skim off the fat from the liquid in the roasting pan and transfer the pan to the stove top. Add the wine and boil it over high heat, stirring to scrape up any sediment from the bottom of the pan. Add the stock, tarragon, honey and salt and boil to reduce the liquid by about half. Strain the gravy into a sauce boat. Carve the guard at the table.

SUGGESTED ACCOMPANIMENTS: *steamed courgettes and carrots; new potatoes.*

EDITOR'S NOTE: *For this recipe, ask your butcher for matching racks — ideally from the same animal.*

Forming a Guard of Honour

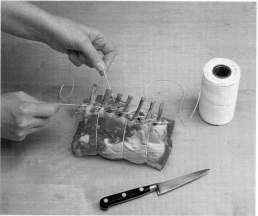

1 INTERLOCKING THE BONE TIPS. Stand up two racks (prepared according to the instructions on page 135), their concave sides facing each other. Press the racks together so that the tips of the bones are interlaced.

2 TYING THE RACKS TOGETHER. Cut three lengths of string, each about 45 cm (18 inches) long. Tie each length round the racks. Cut another piece of string — about 75 cm (30 inches) long — and weave it in and out of the crossed ribs (above) from one end to the other. Bring the ends of the string back along the outside of the crossed ribs and tie them in a knot.

Crown Roast Garnished with Glazed Onions

Serves 7
Working time: about 1 hour
Total time: about 2 hours

Calories **290**
Protein **29g**
Cholesterol **75mg**
Total fat **14g**
Saturated fat **6g**
Sodium **265mg**

2	850 g (1¾ lb) racks of lamb, each with seven cutlets, chine bones removed, bone tips shortened by 5 cm (2 inches), trimmed of fat and prepared for roasting (page 135)	2
¼ tsp	salt	¼ tsp
	freshly ground black pepper	
½ tbsp	virgin olive oil	½ tbsp
1 tbsp	caster sugar	1 tbsp
18	pickling onions, peeled	18
6 tbsp	unsalted chicken stock (recipe, page 137)	6 tbsp
Asparagus stuffing		
500 g	asparagus, washed, trimmed and peeled	1 lb
1 tbsp	virgin olive oil	1 tbsp
1	onion, finely chopped	1
1	garlic clove, crushed	1
90 g	fresh white breadcrumbs	3 oz
2 tbsp	chopped parsley	2 tbsp
1 tsp	finely grated lemon rind	1 tsp
1	egg white	1
¼ tsp	salt	¼ tsp
	freshly ground black pepper	

Assemble the racks for a crown roast following the technique shown opposite. To prevent charring during cooking, cover the exposed bone tips with a single layer of aluminium foil, pressing the foil round the bones. Season the crown with the salt and some pepper; place it in a roasting pan. Preheat the oven to 220°C (425°F or Mark 7).

To make the stuffing, cut off the asparagus tips and set them aside. Cut the stems into thin slices and blanch them in boiling water for 1 minute. Using a slotted spoon, remove the slices to a colander to drain well, then set them aside. Add the asparagus tips to the water and cook them until they are tender — 2 to 3 minutes. Pour them into a colander and refresh them under cold running water. Drain the tips and set them aside.

Heat the oil for the stuffing in a heavy frying pan over medium heat. Add the chopped onion, then reduce the heat to low and cook until the onion is soft but not brown — 6 to 8 minutes. Add the garlic and asparagus stems to the pan and cook for a further 3 minutes. Remove the pan from the heat and stir in the breadcrumbs, parsley, lemon rind and egg white. Season the stuffing with the salt and some pepper and squeeze it gently together.

Fill the centre of the crown with the stuffing. Roast the crown for 10 minutes, then reduce the oven temperature to 180°C (350°F or Mark 4) and continue roasting for 50 to 60 minutes for rare to medium meat.

Fifteen minutes before the crown is ready, prepare the garnish. Heat the oil in a frying pan over moderate heat and sprinkle in the sugar. Heat until the sugar turns to a golden caramel. Add the onions and shake the pan gently until they are evenly coated with the caramel. Reduce the heat to low, add the stock and cover the pan. Cook until the onions are nearly tender — about 8 minutes — then add the asparagus tips. Cook for a further 2 to 3 minutes, until the onions are soft and the asparagus is heated through.

Place the crown on a warm serving dish, and garnish it with the glazed onions and asparagus tips.

SUGGESTED ACCOMPANIMENTS: *julienned carrots; boiled potatoes tossed in parsley.*

Shaping a Crown Roast

1 *FREEING THE RIB BONES. Place two racks (prepared according to the instructions on page 135) concave side up on a work surface. Using a small sharp knife, make 5 mm (¼ inch) deep cuts between the thick end of the rib bones of each of the racks.*

2 *JOINING THE TWO RACKS. Lay the racks end to end. Cut two lengths of string each about 30 cm (12 inches) long. Using a large trussing needle, sew the end rib bones of the two racks together, then knot the string.*

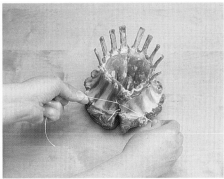

3 *COMPLETING THE CROWN. Gently curve the two racks, concave side out, into semicircles. Cut two or more lengths of string and sew and tie the two free rack ends together to form a circle.*

Chilled Cutlets Coated with Mint Aspic

TO MAKE A CLEAR ASPIC, THE BOWLS, MUSLIN AND COOKING
UTENSILS MUST BE SCRUPULOUSLY CLEAN. HERE EVERYTHING
IS SCALDED TO ENSURE THAT THE LIQUID DOES NOT BECOME
CLOUDED BY IMPURITIES.

Serves 6
Working time: about 1 hour and 15 minutes
Total time: about 4 hours and 30 minutes
(includes cooling and setting)

Calories **255**
Protein **35g**
Cholesterol **75mg**
Total fat **12g**
Saturated fat **6g**
Sodium **230mg**

2	750 g (1 ½ lb) racks of lamb, each with six cutlets, chined, bone tips shortened by 5 cm (2 inches)	2
½ tsp	salt	½ tsp
	shredded lettuce, for garnish	
12	spring onions, cut into brushes, for garnish	12
Mint aspic		
90 cl	unsalted chicken stock (recipe, page 137)	1 ½ pints
3	eggs, whites and shells only	3
45 g	powdered gelatine	1 ½ oz
2 tbsp	red wine vinegar	2 tbsp
4 tbsp	chopped mint	4 tbsp

Preheat the oven to 220°C (425°F or Mark 7). Prepare
the racks for roasting as shown on page 135, and
sprinkle them with the salt. Place the racks in a roasting pan and roast them for 10 minutes, then reduce
the oven temperature to 180°C (350°F or Mark 4) and
continue roasting for a further 30 to 40 minutes for rare
to medium meat. Transfer the lamb to a large plate
and allow it to cool for 1 hour, then refrigerate it for
about 1 hour, until chilled.

Meanwhile, prepare the aspic. Put a large piece of
muslin, a wire balloon whisk and a large metal sieve
into a large saucepan. Fill the saucepan with cold
water and bring it to the boil to scald the contents and
the saucepan. Pour the boiling water into a large
mixing bowl, to scald that also, then pour the water
away. Wring out the muslin. Line the sieve with the
muslin and place it over the mixing bowl.

Put the stock into the saucepan and add the egg
whites, egg shells, gelatine and vinegar. Place the
saucepan over a medium heat and bring the mixture to
the boil, whisking with the balloon whisk until a thick
foam forms on the surface. Stop whisking and allow
the liquid to boil until the foam rises to the top of the
saucepan. At once, remove the saucepan from the
heat and allow the foam to settle back down in the
saucepan. Repeat this process twice more, without
whisking, then remove the saucepan from the heat
and allow it to stand for 10 minutes. Carefully pour the

liquid into the muslin-lined sieve, without allowing the foam to break up. When the liquid has completely drained through, discard the foam. Allow the aspic to cool for about 1 hour, then stir in the mint.

Remove the chine bones from the lamb. Cut down between the ribs to divide each rack into six cutlets. Carefully cut away all the excess fat to leave just the lean eye of the meat attached to the bone. Place the cutlets on a wire rack set over a large clean tray.

Stir the aspic over ice, or refrigerate it, until it begins to thicken. Spoon aspic over each cutlet to coat it evenly. Refrigerate the cutlets for 10 to 15 minutes,

until the aspic has set, then coat them once again. Refrigerate them until the aspic is firmly set — about 20 minutes.

Arrange the cutlets on a bed of shredded lettuce. Serve garnished with the spring onion brushes.

EDITOR'S NOTE: *To make spring onion brushes, trim off the bulb and onion top to leave a 7.5 cm (3 inch) length of firm stalk. Make three or four 2.5 cm (1 inch) long cuts into each end of each onion. Place the spring onions in iced water for about 1 hour, until the ends curl.*

The cutlets may be prepared up to 24 hours in advance and kept in a covered container in the refrigerator.

Chops Stuffed with Walnuts and Parsley

Serves 4
Working time: about 20 minutes
Total time: about 40 minutes

Calories **280**
Protein **23g**
Cholesterol **65mg**
Total fat **14g**
Saturated fat **5g**
Sodium **215mg**

4	loin chops (about 125 g/4 oz each), trimmed of fat	4
2 tsp	safflower oil	2 tsp
1	onion, chopped	1
12.5 cl	unsalted chicken stock (recipe, page 137)	4 fl oz
3 tbsp	currants	3 tbsp
45 g	fresh breadcrumbs	1½ oz
2 tsp	chopped parsley	2 tsp
2 tbsp	finely chopped shelled walnuts	2 tbsp
1 tsp	chopped fresh thyme, or ¼ tsp dried thyme	1 tsp
¼ tsp	salt	¼ tsp
	freshly ground black pepper	

First prepare the stuffing. Heat 1 teaspoon of the oil in a non-stick frying pan over medium heat. Add the onion and cook it until it is translucent — 2 to 3 minutes. Add the stock and currants and bring the liquid to a simmer. Remove the pan from the heat and cover it. Let the mixture stand until the currants have plumped up — about 5 minutes. Stir in the breadcrumbs, parsley, walnuts, thyme, ⅛ teaspoon of the salt and some pepper and set the stuffing aside.

Preheat the oven to 200°C (400°F or Mark 6). Arrange the chops in front of you with the fillet on the right and the apron farthest from you. Insert a small, sharp knife horizontally into each chop in turn on the right-hand side, near the end of the bone that divides the fillet from the eye. Extend the cut towards the eye, but make sure that the knife does not emerge on the far side of the eye. Rotate the knife to create a pocket

within the flesh of the eye. Using a spoon or your fingers, fill the pockets with the stuffing mixture. Fold the long, thin apron of the chop to cover the opening of the pocket, and secure the apron to the fillet with a cocktail stick.

Heat the remaining teaspoon of oil in a shallow fireproof casserole over medium-high heat. Place the stuffed chops in the oil and lightly brown them on one side — 1 to 2 minutes. Turn the chops over and season them with the remaining ⅛ teaspoon of salt and some more pepper. Put the casserole into the oven and bake the chops for 15 to 20 minutes.

Remove the casserole from the oven and let the chops rest in a warm place for 5 minutes. Remove the cocktail sticks before serving.

SUGGESTED ACCOMPANIMENT: *ratatouille.*

Lamb with Hazelnut Sauce

Serves 6
Working (and total) time: about 30 minutes

Calories **175**		
Protein **23g**		
Cholesterol **65mg**		
Total fat **14g**		
Saturated fat **5g**		
Sodium **200mg**		

2	racks of lamb (about 600 g/1 ¼ lb each), boned, the fatty flap of meat that extends from the eye removed	2
45 cl	unsalted brown or chicken stock (recipes, page 137)	¾ pint
12.5 cl	dry white wine	4 fl oz
½ tsp	salt	½ tsp
	freshly ground black pepper	
175 g	turnips, peeled and finely diced	6 oz
60 g	shelled hazelnuts, toasted and chopped	2 oz

Preheat the oven to 230°C (450°F or Mark 8).

To make the sauce, put the stock and wine in a saucepan and boil rapidly until only half of the liquid remains — 8 to 10 minutes. Season with ¼ teaspoon of the salt and some black pepper. Add the turnips to the reduced stock and simmer them until they are just tender — about 5 minutes — then remove the pan from the heat and set it aside.

While the sauce is cooking, brush a heavy frying pan with a little oil. Set the pan over high heat, then quickly seal the meat and transfer it to a roasting pan. Season the meat with the remaining salt and some black pepper. Roast the lamb for 5 to 10 minutes for rare to medium meat.

Just before the meat is ready, return the sauce to the heat. Stir in the chopped hazelnuts and heat the sauce through.

Carve the lamb and arrange slices on six plates. Serve with the sauce spooned over the meat.

SUGGESTED ACCOMPANIMENT: *spinach tagliatelle.*

EDITOR'S NOTE: *To toast hazelnuts, put them on a baking sheet in a preheated 180°C (350°F or Mark 4) oven for 10 minutes.*

Loin with Juniper Berry Sauce

Serves 8
Working time: about 20 minutes
Total time: about 30 minutes

Calories **250**
Protein **25g**
Cholesterol **90mg**
Total fat **12g**
Saturated fat **5g**
Sodium **70mg**

2	loins of lamb (about 1 kg/2 ¼ lb each), boned and trimmed of fat (page 134), fillet reserved for another recipe	2
1 litre	unsalted brown or chicken stock (recipes, page 137)	1¾ pints
30 cl	dry Madeira	½ pint
4 tsp	redcurrant jelly	4 tsp
4 tsp	juniper berries, coarsely crushed with a pestle and mortar	4 tsp
1 tsp	virgin olive oil	1 tsp

Preheat the oven to 220°C (425°F or Mark 7).

Put the stock, Madeira and redcurrant jelly in a heavy-bottomed saucepan and boil them over high heat until the liquid is reduced to about ½ litre (16 fl oz). Add half the juniper berries and continue boiling until the stock has further reduced to about 30 cl (½ pint), then remove the pan from the heat and set it aside.

Meanwhile, brush the eyes of loin with the oil, sprinkle the meat with the remaining juniper berries and place it in a roasting pan. Roast the meat on the middle shelf of the oven for 12 minutes. Turn off the heat and leave the lamb in the pan on the floor of the oven for 10 minutes.

Transfer the lamb to a warmed serving dish, cover the dish and set it aside in a warm place. Skim off any fat from the juices in the pan and pour the remaining juices into the juniper berry sauce. Reheat the sauce, pour some of it round the lamb to moisten it and pour the rest into a warmed sauce boat. Serve immediately.

SUGGESTED ACCOMPANIMENTS: *red cabbage; duchesse potatoes.*

Loin Stuffed with Wild Mushrooms

Serves 4
Working time: about 1 hour
Total time: about 2 hours

Calories **235** Protein **24g** Cholesterol **175mg** Total fat **12g** Saturated fat **4g** Sodium **225mg**	1 kg	loin, boned and trimmed of fat (page 134), eye only	2¼ lb
	30 g	dried wild mushrooms (chanterelle, ceps or shiitake), soaked for 20 minutes in hot water	1 oz
	1 tbsp	virgin olive oil	1 tbsp
	3	spring onions, white parts finely chopped, green tops cut into 2.5 cm (1 inch) pieces	3
	1 tbsp	finely chopped celery	1 tbsp
	2	garlic cloves, finely chopped	2
	2 tsp	fresh thyme, or ¾ tsp dried thyme	2 tsp
	125 g	fresh mushrooms, wiped clean and chopped	4 oz

¼ litre	unsalted brown stock (recipe, page 137)	8 fl oz
1 tbsp	fresh lemon juice	1 tbsp
¼ tsp	salt	¼ tsp
	freshly ground black pepper	

Remove the dried mushrooms from their soaking liquid; cut off and discard any woody or sandy stems. Finely chop the mushrooms and set them aside. Carefully strain the mushroom-soaking liquid through a muslin-lined sieve set over a bowl to remove any grit. Set the bowl aside.

Heat half of the oil in a heavy-bottomed saucepan over medium heat. Add the white parts of the spring onions, the celery, garlic and half of the thyme. Cook the mixture, stirring occasionally, for 3 minutes. Add the reconstituted dried mushrooms and fresh mushrooms to the pan together with 4 tablespoons of the stock, the lemon juice, half of the salt and a generous grinding of pepper. Cover the pan, reduce the heat to low, and cook the mushrooms, stirring them every now and then, until all the liquid has been absorbed — 20 to 25 minutes. Transfer the mushroom stuffing to a bowl, and let it cool to room temperature.

Preheat the oven to 220°C (425°F or Mark 7). To butterfly the eye of loin and prepare it for stuffing, cut it in half horizontally, leaving the halves hinged at one side. Open out the meat and spread the stuffing down the centre. Fold the halves back together and tie the meat securely. Place the meat in a heavy roasting pan and brush it with the remaining oil. Roast the lamb for about 25 minutes for medium meat.

Remove the pan from the oven and set the lamb aside on a carving board while you prepare the sauce. Skim off the fat from the pan, leaving behind any caramelized juices. Place the pan over medium heat. Pour the strained mushroom liquid and the remaining stock into the pan, stirring well with a wooden spoon to dissolve the caramelized juices in the bottom. Stir in the remaining salt, the remaining thyme, the green spring onion tops and some pepper. Boil the liquid until about 12.5 cl (4 fl oz) of sauce remains — about 10 minutes.

Cut the lamb into 12 slices and arrange them on a serving dish or on individual plates. Pour the sauce over the slices and serve immediately.

SUGGESTED ACCOMPANIMENTS: *peas; French bread.*

EDITOR'S NOTE: *Only the eye of the loin is used here; reserve the fillet for another recipe where lean meat is called for.*

Loin on a Bed of Green Leaves

ASK THE BUTCHER TO SAW THROUGH THE CHINE BONE OF THE
LOINS TO MAKE IT EASIER TO CARVE THE MEAT

Serves 8
Working time: about 40 minutes
Total time: about 1 hour and 45 minutes

Calories **235**
Protein **24g**
Cholesterol **75mg**
Total fat **12g**
Saturated fat **4g**
Sodium **195mg**

2	loins (about 1 kg/2 ¼ lb each), trimmed of fat	2
1 tbsp	virgin olive oil	1 tbsp
1 tbsp	grainy mustard	1 tbsp
⅛ tsp	salt	⅛ tsp
	freshly ground black pepper	
2	garlic cloves, finely chopped	2
25 g	fresh wholemeal breadcrumbs	¾ oz
1 tbsp	chopped parsley	1 tbsp
1 tsp	chopped fresh thyme, or ¼ tsp dried thyme	1 tsp
1 tsp	chopped fresh rosemary, or ¼ tsp dried rosemary, crumbled	1 tsp
Wilted green leaf salad		
1 tbsp	virgin olive oil	1 tbsp
2	spring onions, trimmed and chopped	2
500 g	dandelion greens or spinach, stemmed, washed and dried	1 lb
1	bunch watercress, trimmed, washed and dried	1
16	cherry tomatoes, halved	16
1 tbsp	red wine vinegar	1 tbsp
⅛ tsp	salt	⅛ tsp
	freshly ground black pepper	

Put the lamb in a roasting pan bone side down. In a small bowl, combine 1 teaspoon of the oil, the mustard, salt, some pepper and half of the garlic. Rub this mixture over the lamb and let it stand at room temperature for 1 hour.

Preheat the oven to 220°C (425°F or Mark 7). Roast the lamb until it has browned — 25 to 35 minutes for rare to medium meat.

Mix together the breadcrumbs, parsley, thyme, rosemary, the remaining garlic and some pepper. Sprinkle the breadcrumb mixture over the top of the lamb; dribble the remaining 2 teaspoons of oil over the breadcrumbs. Continue roasting the lamb until the breadcrumbs have browned — about 10 minutes more. Keep the lamb warm while you make the salad.

For the salad, heat the oil in a heavy frying pan or sauté pan over medium-high heat. Add the spring onions and sauté them for 45 seconds, then add the greens, watercress, tomatoes and vinegar. Toss the vegetables until the greens are slightly wilted — about 30 seconds. Remove the pan from the heat and season the salad with the salt and some pepper.

Carve the lamb into 16 pieces and serve them on beds of salad.

SUGGESTED ACCOMPANIMENTS: *parslied potatoes; bread rolls.*

2 *Toasted walnuts, added 5 minutes before the end of cooking, lend a crunch to lean lamb and vegetables gently simmered in a wine and anchovy sauce (recipe, pa*

Simmering for Flavour

Slow cooking in liquid is the traditional way of tenderizing firmer, more gelatinous cuts of lamb. In time, tough meat yields almost magically, but since the cuts usually selected for moist cooking — shoulder, neck and breast — are high in fat, many health-conscious cooks avoid moist methods for lamb. This chapter demonstrates that they need not. Lean, tender cuts from the leg or loin, normally associated with dry cooking, respond as well to moist cooking as the fattier cuts. And fattier cuts can be rescued for the healthy table by a scrupulous degreasing process.

Braising and stewing involve the same techniques, but while the pieces of meat for braising are usually quite large, meat for stewing is usually cut into small pieces before cooking. In either case, the meat is often first seared in a heavy pan. The liquid then makes a distinctive contribution of its own: stock, wine, beer or tomatoes can all enhance the flavour of the lamb. Accompanying vegetables may be cooked with the meat from the beginning for a rewarding exchange of flavours — as in the lamb dhansak on page 68 — or added in stages to maintain their individual tastes and textures — as in the navarin on page 72. At the end of cooking, the braising liquid serves as a sauce. Poaching, another method of moist cooking, uses more liquid than braising, and the poaching liquid may appear as a soup at another meal.

Because lean, prime cuts from the leg or loin have less muscle and connective tissue than conventional stewing lamb, cooking times are shorter. While a conventional stew may take 2 to 3 hours to cook, most of the recipes here require little more than an hour. Whatever the quality of the meat, however, moist cooking is slow cooking, since meat that is boiled becomes tough. Keep the liquid to the gentlest of simmers. A striking exception to this rule is the Mongolian hot pot (page 86), in which thin strips of loin, plunged into boiling stock at the dining table, cook in seconds — too quickly to become stringy.

Even lean lamb will leave a trace of fat on the surface of a stew after simmering for an hour. This should be skimmed off with a spoon or paper towels before serving. And if you prepare a dish in advance and remove the fat when it has cooled and solidified, you degrease even more effectively — so thoroughly that you can afford to use such cuts as shoulder or neck. In the navarin (page 72), cubes of shoulder are partly cooked, then refrigerated for at least 4 hours, when the solid crust of surface fat is lifted off and discarded before the recipe is completed. Most of the recipes in this chapter can be adapted for traditional stewing lamb by following this chilling and degreasing procedure, and extending the cooking time by an hour or so.

Moroccan Spiced Stew

SINCE MEDIEVAL TIMES, SPICED STEWS OF MEAT
AND PRUNES HAVE BEEN POPULAR STAPLES OF THE
NORTH AFRICAN DIET.

Serves 4
Working time: about 30 minutes
Total time: about 1 hour and 45 minutes

Calories **315**
Protein **36g**
Cholesterol **80mg**
Total fat **14g**
Saturated fat **4g**
Sodium **175mg**

500 g	lean lamb (from the leg), trimmed of fat and cut into 2.5 cm (1 inch) cubes	1 lb
½ tsp	safflower oil	½ tsp
350 g	pickling onions	12 oz
45 cl	unsalted brown or chicken stock (recipes, page 137)	¾ pint
1 tbsp	clear honey	1 tbsp
1 tsp	ground cinnamon	1 tsp
½ tsp	saffron threads	½ tsp
½ tsp	ground ginger	½ tsp
¼ tsp	grated nutmeg	¼ tsp
½	orange, grated rind and juice	½
12	ready-to-eat stoned prunes	12
30 g	blanched almonds	1 oz
¼ tsp	salt	¼ tsp
	freshly ground black pepper	

Heat the oil in a non-stick frying pan over medium-high heat and sauté the onions until they are golden-brown — about 5 minutes. Transfer them to a bowl and set them aside.

Add the lamb cubes to the frying pan and brown them for 2 to 3 minutes. Transfer them to a large, heavy-bottomed saucepan or fireproof casserole.

Pour off any fat from the frying pan, then add the stock and bring it to the boil, stirring with a wooden spoon to dislodge any deposits from the bottom of the pan. Pour the boiling stock over the lamb. Add the honey, cinnamon, saffron, ginger and nutmeg to the casserole, cover and simmer for 30 minutes.

Add the onions, orange rind and juice to the lamb and simmer for a further 30 minutes. Finally add the prunes, almonds and salt, season with pepper and simmer, uncovered, for 15 minutes.

SUGGESTED ACCOMPANIMENT: *couscous.*

EDITOR'S NOTE: *The prunes used in this recipe are sold for eating straight from the packet and do not require presoaking or stoning. If you use ordinary dried prunes, soak them in cold water for 3 hours and stone them before cooking.*

Braised Lamb with Mango

Serves 4
Working time: about 30 minutes
Total time: about 7 hours and 30 minutes
(includes marinating)

Calories **300**
Protein **45g**
Cholesterol **75mg**
Total fat **10g**
Saturated fat **4g**
Sodium **320mg**

500 g	lamb slices, cut from the fillet end of the leg, trimmed of fat and cut into 7.5 cm (3 inch) long strips	1 lb
30 cl	plain low-fat yogurt	½ pint
1 tsp	finely chopped fresh ginger root	1 tsp
1 tbsp	ground coriander	1 tbsp
1 tsp	ground cumin	1 tsp
2 tsp	safflower oil	2 tsp
1	onion, finely sliced	1
1	garlic clove, crushed	1
2 tsp	coriander seeds, crushed	2 tsp
1 tbsp	cornflour	1 tbsp
12.5 cl	unsalted chicken stock (recipe, page 137)	4 fl oz
1	bay leaf	1
⅛ tsp	powdered saffron or turmeric	⅛ tsp
¾ tsp	salt	¾ tsp
2	mangoes	2
4	large fresh coriander leaves	4

Mix together the yogurt, ginger, ground coriander and cumin, then stir in the strips of lamb, coating them in the mixture. Cover the meat and leave it to marinate in the refrigerator for at least 6 hours, or overnight.

In a heavy-bottomed fireproof casserole, heat the oil and stir in the onion and garlic. Cook them over low heat for 1 minute, then add the crushed coriander seeds and sauté until the seeds begin to pop. Mix the cornflour with a tablespoon of the lamb marinade. Stir the cornflour mixture into the rest of the marinade. Transfer the meat and its marinade to the casserole and continue cooking gently for 1 minute. Add the stock, bay leaf, saffron or turmeric, and salt. Cover the casserole and simmer the stew over low heat until the meat is tender — about 1 hour.

Peel the mangoes; cut two thin slices from one of them and reserve these for a garnish. Remove the stones and cut the flesh into 1 cm (½ inch) cubes. Add the mango cubes to the lamb and simmer the casserole over low heat for a further 5 minutes.

Just before serving, coarsely chop the coriander leaves and sprinkle them over the lamb. Serve it garnished with the reserved slices of mango.

SUGGESTED ACCOMPANIMENT: *chapatis; boiled rice.*

Lamb Dhansak

THE PARSEES, WHO MOVED FROM PERSIA TO SETTLE IN INDIA IN
THE EIGHTH CENTURY A.D., BROUGHT WITH THEM THE DHANSAK:
A MILDLY SPICED STEW OF MEAT AND LENTILS.

Serves 4
Working time: about 50 minutes
Total time: about 10 hours (includes soaking)

Calories **285**
Protein **35g**
Cholesterol **75mg**
Total fat **8g**
Saturated fat **4g**
Sodium **340mg**

500 g	lean lamb (from the leg), trimmed of fat and cut into 2.5 cm (1 inch) cubes	1 lb
1	large onion, finely chopped	1
2 tsp	ground coriander	2 tsp
2 tsp	ground cumin	2 tsp
1 tsp	ground cinnamon	1 tsp
1 tsp	ground cardamom	1 tsp
1 tsp	ground turmeric	1 tsp
1 tsp	black peppercorns	1 tsp
20 cl	plain low-fat yogurt	7 fl oz
2	garlic cloves, crushed	2
2	fresh hot green chili peppers, finely chopped (caution, page 83)	2
2.5 cm	piece fresh ginger root, finely chopped	1 inch
250 g	mixed lentils, washed, soaked for 8 hours or overnight, drained	8 oz
350 g	aubergine, trimmed and cut into 2.5 cm (1 inch) cubes	12 oz
250 g	butternut squash, peeled and cut into 2.5 cm (1 inch) cubes	8 oz
350 g	tomatoes, finely chopped	12 oz
150 g	fresh spinach, thoroughly washed and torn into small pieces	5 oz
½ tsp	salt	½ tsp
3 tbsp	finely chopped fresh coriander	3 tbsp

Brush a large fireproof casserole or heavy-bottomed saucepan with oil. Add the onion and cook it over medium-high heat, stirring constantly, until it is softened — about 2 to 3 minutes. Stir in the lamb, ground coriander, cumin, cinnamon, cardamom, turmeric and peppercorns, then add 1 tablespoon of the yogurt. Cook over high heat, turning the meat until the yogurt is completely absorbed — 3 to 5 minutes. Add the rest of the yogurt, 1 tablespoon at a time, stirring constantly after each addition until all of the yogurt is absorbed.

Stir in the garlic, chopped chili peppers and ginger, and cook for a further 1 minute. Add the lentils, aubergine, squash, tomatoes and spinach and pour in just enough water to cover the ingredients. Bring the mixture to the boil, then reduce the heat to low, cover and simmer until the lamb is tender — about 1 hour. Check the pan from time to time and add a little more water if the stew becomes dry. About 10 minutes before the end of cooking, add the salt and 2 tablespoons of the fresh coriander.

Lift out the meat and about half of the vegetable and lentil mixture with a slotted spoon and set it aside. Using a potato masher, mash the lentil and vegetable mixture left in the pan, then reincorporate the meat and the rest of the lentil and vegetable mixture and gently reheat it. Serve garnished with the remaining tablespoon of coriander.

SUGGESTED ACCOMPANIMENT: *naan bread; basmati rice.*

EDITOR'S NOTE: *Oriental food shops generally stock several varieties of lentils. The mixture suggested for this recipe is channa dal, toor dal and masoor dal, but other varieties can be used instead.*

Lamb with Puréed Asparagus and Jerusalem Artichokes

Serves 6
Working time: about 1 hour
Total time: about 2 hours and 30 minutes

Calories **225**
Protein **30g**
Cholesterol **80mg**
Total fat **9g**
Saturated fat **4g**
Sodium **270mg**

750 g	lean lamb (from the leg or loin), trimmed of fat and cut into 7.5 cm (3 inch) strips	1½ lb
500 g	asparagus, trimmed and peeled	1 lb
1 tsp	salt	1 tsp
½ tbsp	safflower oil	½ tbsp
3	shallots, halved	3
500g	Jerusalem artichokes	1 lb
4 tsp	fresh lemon juice	4 tsp
60 g	watercress, washed, trimmed, blanched for 30 seconds and chopped	2 oz
¼ tsp	white pepper	¼ tsp
3 tbsp	thick Greek yogurt	3 tbsp

Cut off the tips of the asparagus spears and set them aside. Cook the stems in boiling water to cover, with half a teaspoon of the salt, until they are soft — about 15 minutes. Remove the stems with a slotted spoon, drain them and set them aside; strain and reserve the cooking liquid.

While the asparagus is cooking, heat the oil in a frying pan, add the shallots and soften them over a medium heat — about 5 minutes. Transfer the shallots to a fireproof casserole. Increase the heat under the frying pan and lightly brown the lamb strips in two batches, transferring each batch to the casserole. Pour the reserved asparagus cooking liquid over the meat and shallots. The liquid should cover the lamb; if necessary, add extra water. Simmer the casserole until the meat is tender — about 1 hour.

Meanwhile, cook the artichokes. Put 1 teaspoon of the lemon juice into a non-reactive pan with 1 litre (1¾ pints) of water. Peel and chop the artichokes, dropping them into the water immediately to prevent discoloration. Bring the water to the boil and cook the artichokes until tender — 20 to 30 minutes. Drain the artichokes and purée them in a blender. Purée and sieve the asparagus stems. Set the purées aside.

Skim off any fat from the casserole and remove the meat and shallots. Bring the liquid in the casserole to the boil, then add the asparagus tips and cook gently until they are just tender — about 5 minutes. Remove the tips with a slotted spoon and keep them warm.

Stir the asparagus and artichoke purées and the watercress into the cooking liquid to make a sauce. Gently heat the sauce and season it with the remaining lemon juice and salt and the white pepper. Return the meat to the sauce and heat it through gently. Add the asparagus tips and swirl the yogurt on the top. Serve at once.

SUGGESTED ACCOMPANIMENT: *mixed wild and white rice.*

Indian Lamb with Spinach

Serves 6
Working time: about 50 minutes
Total time: about 2 hours

Calories **275**
Protein **37g**
Cholesterol **75mg**
Total fat **9g**
Saturated fat **4g**
Sodium **400mg**

500 g	lean lamb (from the leg), trimmed of fat and cut into 2.5 cm (1 inch) cubes	1 lb
1	large onion, finely chopped	1
4 tsp	ground coriander	4 tsp
1 tbsp	mustard seeds	1 tbsp
2 tsp	ground cumin	2 tsp
1 tsp	chili powder	1 tsp
1 tsp	ground turmeric	1 tsp
20 cl	plain low-fat yogurt	7 fl oz
2.5 cm	piece fresh ginger root, finely chopped	1 inch
3	garlic cloves, crushed	3
1 kg	fresh spinach, trimmed, thoroughly washed and torn into small pieces	2 lb
¼ tsp	salt	¼ tsp

Brush a heavy, non-stick fireproof casserole or saucepan with oil, add the onion and soften it over medium-high heat for 2 to 3 minutes, stirring constantly. Stir in the lamb cubes, coriander, mustard seeds, cumin, chili powder and turmeric and mix all the ingredients thoroughly together. Add 1 tablespoon of the yogurt and cook over high heat, stirring the meat continuously until all of the yogurt is absorbed — 3 to 5 minutes. Add the rest of the yogurt, 1 tablespoon at a time, stirring constantly after each addition until the yogurt is completely absorbed.

Stir in the ginger and garlic, add just enough water to cover the meat and bring the liquid to the boil. Cover the casserole, reduce the heat and simmer until the lamb is tender — about 1 hour.

When the meat is cooked, increase the heat to medium and add the spinach in batches, stirring each batch until it is wilted. When all the spinach is incorporated cook the stew, uncovered, over high heat to evaporate any excess liquid — about 5 minutes. Add the salt just before serving.

SUGGESTED ACCOMPANIMENTS: *poppadoms; saffron rice; Indian chutney or relish.*

Lamb and Apple Casserole

Serves 4
Working time: about 30 minutes
Total time: about 2 hours and 25 minutes

Calories **430**
Protein **40g**
Cholesterol **75mg**
Total fat **10g**
Saturated fat **5g**
Sodium **290mg**

500 g	lean lamb (from the loin), trimmed of fat and cut into thin slices	1 lb
750 g	potatoes, very thinly sliced	1 ½ lb
2 tsp	finely chopped fresh sage, or ½ tsp dried sage	2 tsp
1	orange, finely grated rind and juice	1
½ tsp	salt	½ tsp
	freshly ground black pepper	
600 g	dessert apples, peeled, cored and sliced	1 ¼ lb
1	large onion, sliced into very thin rings	1
15 cl	dry cider	¼ pint

Preheat the oven to 180°C (350°F or Mark 4). Arrange half of the potato slices in the bottom of a 2.5 litre (4 pint) casserole. Sprinkle them with a little of the sage, orange rind and salt, and plenty of black pepper.

Cover the potatoes with half the apple slices; season this layer in the same way.

Continue to build up the casserole in layers as follows, seasoning each layer with some of the sage, orange rind, salt and pepper. Arrange the slices of lamb evenly over the apple, and spread the onion rings over the lamb, leaving a small space uncovered in the centre of the layer. Cover the onion with the remaining apples, and top the casserole with the remaining potatoes, maintaining the small gap in the centre of both layers and overlapping the slices of potato on the top layer in neat concentric circles.

Mix the orange juice and cider together and pour the liquid slowly into the hole in the centre of the potato topping. Cover and cook the casserole in the oven for 1½ hours, then remove the lid and continue cooking until the ingredients feel tender when pierced with a fine skewer and the potato topping is golden-brown — 30 to 45 minutes. Serve the casserole hot, straight from the dish.

SUGGESTED ACCOMPANIMENT: *purple-sprouting broccoli.*

Navarin with Mustard Croûtons

THIS CLASSIC FRENCH STEW OF LAMB AND YOUNG
VEGETABLES IS COOKED SEVERAL HOURS IN ADVANCE SO THAT
ALL EXCESS FAT CAN RISE TO THE SURFACE AND THEN
BE EASILY DISCARDED.

Serves 4
Working time: about 45 minutes
Total time: about 7 hours (includes chilling)

Calories **430**
Protein **35g**
Cholesterol **75mg**
Total fat **9g**
Saturated fat **4g**
Sodium **600mg**

500 g	lean stewing lamb, trimmed of fat and cut into 2 cm (¾ inch) cubes	1 lb
1 tbsp	plain flour	1 tbsp
60 cl	unsalted brown or chicken stock (recipes, page 137)	1 pint
1	onion, sliced	1
2 tbsp	tomato paste	2 tbsp
2	fresh bay leaves	2
1 tsp	chopped fresh thyme, or ¼ tsp dried thyme	1 tsp
¼ tsp	salt	¼ tsp
	freshly ground black pepper	
250 g	turnips, peeled	8 oz
250 g	tiny new potatoes, scrubbed	8 oz
250 g	courgettes	8 oz
250 g	cherry tomatoes, skinned, or large tomatoes, skinned and quartered	8 oz
1	small baguette (about 35 cm/ 14 inches long)	1
2	garlic cloves	2
4 tsp	grainy mustard	4 tsp

Preheat the oven to 190°C (375°F or Mark 5). Toss the meat in the flour. Heat a fireproof casserole over a high heat and add the meat, stirring until the cubes are seared on all sides. Stir in the stock, onion, tomato paste, bay leaves, thyme, salt and some pepper. Bring the mixture to the boil. Cover the casserole, transfer it to the oven and cook it for 50 minutes.

Cut the turnips into 2.5 cm (1 inch) pieces, then use a potato peeler to pare down their sharp edges, giving the pieces an attractive rounded shape. Add the turnips and potatoes to the casserole and return it to the oven for a further 50 minutes. Remove the casserole from the oven, allow the stew to cool, then transfer it to a bowl and refrigerate it until a layer of fat forms on the surface — 4 hours or overnight.

Preheat the oven to 190°C (375°F or Mark 5). Lift off and discard the layer of fat, remove the bay leaves and transfer the stew to a clean casserole. Prepare the courgettes in the same way as the turnips and stir them into the casserole with the tomatoes. Cut the baguette diagonally into 1 cm (½ inch) slices. Halve the cloves of garlic and rub their cut surfaces all over the bread. Spread one side of the bread slices with mustard and arrange them, mustard side up, around the edge of the casserole. Cook the navarin, uncovered, until it is heated through and the bread is crisp — about 25 minutes.

Meatballs with Lentils

Serves 6
Working time: about 45 minutes
Total time: about 1 hour and 30 minutes

Calories **280**	600 g	lean lamb (from the leg or loin), trimmed of fat and minced (page 43)	1 ¼ lb
Protein **25g**	4 tbsp	dry breadcrumbs	4 tbsp
Cholesterol **50mg**	2 tbsp	freshly grated Parmesan cheese	2 tbsp
Total fat **8g**	1 tbsp	chopped fresh rosemary, or 1 tsp dried rosemary, crumbled	1 tbsp
Saturated fat **3g**	2 tsp	virgin olive oil	2 tsp
Sodium **205mg**	1	turnip, chopped	1
	1	onion, chopped	1
	2	carrots, chopped	2
	2	sticks celery, chopped	2
	250 g	fresh mushrooms, wiped clean and thinly sliced	8 oz
	4	garlic cloves, finely chopped	4
	½ tsp	hot red pepper flakes	½ tsp
	200 g	lentils, picked over	7 oz
	⅛ tsp	salt	⅛ tsp
	¾ litre	unsalted chicken stock (recipe, page 137)	1 ¼ pints

Mix together the lamb, breadcrumbs, cheese and rosemary. With your hands, form the mixture into 12 balls. Heat the oil in a large, non-stick or heavy sauté pan set over high heat. Add the meatballs and brown them all over — 4 to 5 minutes. Remove the meatballs from the pan with a slotted spoon and set them aside.

Add the turnip, onion, carrots, celery, mushrooms, garlic and red pepper flakes to the pan. Reduce the heat to low and sauté the vegetables until they are soft — about 8 minutes.

Increase the heat to medium high. Add the lentils, salt and stock, and bring the liquid to the boil. Add the meatballs, cover the pan, leaving the lid slightly ajar, and reduce the heat. Simmer the meatballs and lentils until the lentils are tender — about 45 minutes.

Serve the meatballs and lentils piping hot.

SUGGESTED ACCOMPANIMENT: *radicchio salad.*

Loin Chops with Broad Beans

Serves 4
Working time: about 15 minutes
Total time: about 30 minutes

Calories **290**
Protein **31g**
Cholesterol **75mg**
Total fat **14g**
Saturated fat **6g**
Sodium **255mg**

4	loin chops (about 150 g/5oz each), trimmed of fat	4
	freshly ground black pepper	
2 tsp	safflower oil	2 tsp
30 g	prosciutto or other dry-cured ham, sliced paper thin and cut into narrow strips	1 oz
1	onion, finely chopped	1
2	garlic cloves, finely chopped	2
400 g	canned whole tomatoes, seeded and coarsely chopped, with their juice	14 oz
2 tbsp	chopped fresh basil, or 2 tsp dried basil	2 tbsp
1 tsp	red wine vinegar	1 tsp
300 g	fresh shelled or frozen broad beans	10 oz
1/8 tsp	salt	1/8 tsp

Season the loin chops with pepper. Heat the oil in a heavy sauté pan set over medium-high heat. Add the chops and sear them on both sides — about 1 minute per side. Transfer the chops to a plate. Add the prosciutto and onion to the pan, reduce the heat to medium and cook the mixture, stirring frequently, until the onions have become translucent — about 4 minutes. Add the garlic and cook the mixture for 1 minute more.

Return the chops to the sauté pan and then add the canned tomatoes and their juice, the chopped basil, vinegar, broad beans and salt; bring the mixture to a simmer. Partially cover the pan, and simmer the mixture until the chops are firm yet slightly springy to the touch — about 10 minutes.

Serve the lamb and vegetables at once.

SUGGESTED ACCOMPANIMENT: *tagliatelle tossed with chives.*

Port Paupiettes

Serves 8
Working time: about 1 hour
Total time: about 2 hours

Calories **220**
Protein **27g**
Cholesterol **75mg**
Total fat**8g**
Saturated fat **4g**
Sodium **215mg**

8	lamb slices (about 90 g/3 oz each) cut from the fillet end of the leg, trimmed of fat and flattened (page 24)	8
250 g	lean lamb (from the leg or loin), trimmed of fat and minced (page 43)	8 oz
125 g	canned tomatoes, drained and seeded	4 oz
2 tbsp	chopped fresh tarragon, or 2 tsp dried tarragon	2 tbsp
¼ tsp	freshly ground black pepper	¼ tsp
¾ tsp	salt	¾ tsp
1 tsp	virgin olive oil	1 tsp
15 cl	ruby port	¼ pint
30 cl	unsalted brown stock (recipe, page 137)	½ pint
6	black peppercorns	6
6	garlic cloves, unpeeled	6
1 tsp	arrowroot	1 tsp
2 tbsp	tomato paste	2 tbsp

Mix together the minced lamb with the tomatoes, tarragon, black pepper and ½ teaspoon of the salt. Distribute this mixture among the flattened slices of lamb and roll up each slice to form a paupiette. Secure each paupiette in three or four places with string.

Preheat the oven to 170°C (325°F or Mark 3). Heat the olive oil in a large, heavy frying pan over medium heat until it is hot but not smoking. Sear the paupiettes, turning them until they are evenly browned. Remove the paupiettes from the pan and place them in a shallow casserole.

Increase the heat under the frying pan to high and pour in half of the port. Bring it to the boil and allow it to bubble for a minute, while scraping loose any meat deposits in the pan. Add the brown stock to the port and bring it to the boil. Pour the hot liquid over the paupiettes. Add the black peppercorns and garlic, cover the casserole and cook in the oven until the lamb is completely tender when pierced with a thin skewer — about 1 hour.

Transfer the paupiettes to a cutting board, remove the string and slice each paupiette into five pieces. Arrange the pieces in a heated serving dish and keep them warm while you make the sauce.

Strain the stock through a fine sieve into a wide saucepan and discard the garlic and peppercorns. Add the remaining port and boil the liquid over a high heat until it is reduced by one third and slightly syrupy — about 5 minutes. Mix the arrowroot with 1 tablespoon of water and add it to the sauce. Continue boiling until the sauce clears — 2 to 3 minutes. Add the remaining ¼ teaspoon of salt, remove the sauce from the heat and stir in the tomato paste. Serve the paupiettes immediately with the hot sauce.

SUGGESTED ACCOMPANIMENT: *steamed white cabbage with thyme and parsley.*

Old-Fashioned Lamb and Celery

Serves 8
Working time: about 45 minutes
Total time: about 1 hour and 30 minutes

Calories **325**
Protein **33g**
Cholesterol **90mg**
Total fat **13g**
Saturated fat **4g**
Sodium **225mg**

1 kg	lean lamb (from the leg or loin), trimmed of fat and cut into 2.5 cm (1 inch) cubes	2 lb
60 cl	unsalted chicken or veal stock (recipes, page 137)	1 pint
500 g	baby onions, peeled	1 lb
500 g	button mushrooms, wiped and trimmed	1 lb
8	sticks celery, sliced	8
2 tbsp	cornflour	2 tbsp
60 cl	red wine	1 pint
2	fresh rosemary sprigs	2
8	anchovy fillets, drained, dried on paper towels and finely chopped	8
	freshly ground black pepper	
16	shelled walnut halves, toasted	16

Heat a large non-stick frying pan and quickly brown the cubes of meat on all sides. Transfer the meat to a fireproof casserole, add the stock and simmer, covered, for 30 minutes.

Meanwhile, dry-fry the onions in the frying pan over medium heat for 1 minute. Add the mushrooms and celery and continue cooking, stirring frequently, until the vegetables are golden — 3 to 4 minutes.

Mix the cornflour with a little of the red wine and stir this into the stock in the casserole. Add the rest of the wine and bring the liquid to the boil, stirring all the time. Add the dry-fried vegetables, together with the rosemary sprigs, chopped anchovies and some pepper, then cover the casserole and simmer the stew until the meat is tender — about 45 minutes.

About 5 minutes before the end of the cooking time, stir in the toasted walnut halves. There should be just enough liquid left to cover the meat; if there is too much liquid, transfer some of it to a saucepan over a high heat, reduce it, then return it to the casserole. Serve the stew hot.

SUGGESTED ACCOMPANIMENT: *baked potatoes.*

EDITOR'S NOTE: *To toast walnuts, place them on a baking sheet in a 180°C (350°F or Mark 4) oven for 10 minutes.*

Braised Steaks with a Pumpkin Purée

Serves 4
Working time: about 30 minutes
Total time: about 2 hours and 15 minutes

Calories **370**			
Protein **30g**	4	boneless lamb steaks (about 125 g/4 oz each), cut from the fillet end of the leg, trimmed of fat	4
Cholesterol **90mg**			
Total fat **13g**	1 tsp	safflower oil	1 tsp
Saturated fat **5g**	½ tsp	saffron threads	½ tsp
Sodium **370mg**	¼ tsp	sea salt	¼ tsp
	30 cl	unsalted chicken stock (recipe, page 137)	½ pint
	1 kg	pumpkin, peeled and cut into 4 cm (1½ inch) cubes	2 lb
	4	fresh oregano sprigs	4
	½ tsp	salt	½ tsp
	¼ tsp	white pepper	¼ tsp
	4 tbsp	thick Greek yogurt, mixed with 1 tbsp water	4 tbsp
	30 g	shelled walnuts, quartered and toasted, for garnish	1 oz
		fresh oregano leaves, for garnish	

Secure the steaks with short skewers to form neat rounds. Heat the oil in a wide, heavy frying pan over high heat and brown the steak for about 5 minutes. Transfer the meat to a large fireproof casserole.

Grind the saffron with the sea salt using a pestle and mortar. Bring the stock to the boil, dissolve the saffron and salt in the stock and pour it over the meat in the casserole. Add the pumpkin and the oregano sprigs to the casserole and simmer, partly covered, over very low heat until the meat is tender — about 1¾ hours. From time to time, remove any scum or fat which has risen to the surface.

Lift the steaks out of the casserole and remove the skewers; keep the steaks warm while preparing the sauce. Discard the oregano. Purée the pumpkin with a little of the stock in a blender or food processor, then blend in the remaining stock. Reheat the pumpkin purée and season it with the ½ teaspoon of salt and the pepper. Spoon it on to four warm plates and place a steak in the centre of each. Drop small spoonfuls of yogurt into the purée surrounding the meat and draw a pattern using the technique shown on page 118. Garnish with the walnuts and oregano leaves.

SUGGESTED ACCOMPANIMENT: *basmati rice.*

EDITOR'S NOTE: *To toast walnuts, place them on a baking sheet in a 180°C (350°F or Mark 4) oven for 10 minutes.*

Mexican Lamb

IN THIS DISH, LAMB IS PAIRED WITH A VERSION OF THE
MEXICAN MOLE POBLANO, A SPICY CONCOCTION
FEATURING CHILI PEPPERS AND CHOCOLATE.

Serves 8
Working time: about 45 minutes
Total time: about 1 hour and 45 minutes

Calories **220**
Protein **24g**
Cholesterol **75mg**
Total fat **11g**
Saturated fat **3g**
Sodium **210mg**

1.25 kg	lean lamb (from the leg or loin), trimmed of fat and cut into 1 cm (½ inch) cubes	2½ lb
2 tbsp	virgin olive oil	2 tbsp
5	garlic cloves, finely chopped	5
1	fresh hot green chili pepper, seeded, deribbed and finely chopped (caution, page 83)	1
1 tsp	cumin seeds	1 tsp
1	onion, cut into 1 cm (½ inch) cubes	1
1	sweet green pepper, seeded, deribbed and cut into 1 cm (½ inch) pieces	1
2	large ripe tomatoes, skinned, seeded and cut into 1 cm (½ inch) pieces	2
¼ litre	unsalted brown or chicken stock (recipes, page 137)	8 fl oz
½ tsp	salt	½ tsp
¼ tsp	grated nutmeg	¼ tsp
1½ tbsp	cocoa powder	1½ tbsp

Heat 1 tablespoon of the olive oil in a large, heavy sauté pan set over high heat. Add half of the lamb cubes and sauté them until they are browned on all sides — 5 to 7 minutes. With a slotted spoon, remove the cubes from the pan and transfer them to a bowl. Return the pan to the heat; pour in ½ tablespoon of the remaining oil, and brown the rest of the lamb cubes. Set them aside also.

Add the remaining ½ tablespoon of oil to the pan and return it to the heat. Add the chopped garlic, chili pepper and cumin seeds, and cook the mixture until the garlic is lightly browned — about 1 minute. Add the onion cubes, sweet green pepper, tomatoes, stock, salt and grated nutmeg, and bring the mixture to a simmer. Return the lamb cubes and their juices to the sauté pan, then stir in the cocoa powder. Simmer the stew, stirring occasionally, until the meat is very tender and the sauce has thickened — about 1 hour. Remove the stew from the heat and let it stand for about 10 minutes before serving.

SUGGESTED ACCOMPANIMENT: *corn tortillas*.

Lamb Shank with Chick-Peas

Serves 6
Working time: about 30 minutes
Total time: about 3 hours and 20 minutes (includes soaking)

Calories **240**		
Protein **25g**		
Cholesterol **50mg**		
Total fat **6g**		
Saturated fat **2g**		
Sodium **185mg**		

1.25 kg	leg of lamb, shank end, trimmed of fat	2 ½ lb
500 g	dried chick-peas, picked over	8 oz
½ litre	unsalted brown or chicken stock (recipes, page 137)	16 fl oz
¼ tsp	salt	¼ tsp
	freshly ground black pepper	
¾ tsp	ground coriander	¾ tsp
1	onion, quartered	1
3	garlic cloves, thinly sliced	3
1 tbsp	tomato paste	1 tbsp
1 ½ tsp	fresh thyme, or 1/2 tsp dried thyme	1 ½ tsp
1 tbsp	fresh lemon juice	1 tbsp

Rinse the chick-peas under cold running water, then put them into a large, heavy-bottomed saucepan, and pour in enough water to cover them by about 7.5 cm (3 inches). Cover the pan, leaving the lid ajar, and slowly bring the liquid to the boil over medium-low heat. Boil the chick-peas for 2 minutes, then turn off the heat and soak them, covered, for at least 1 hour.

Meanwhile, place the lamb in a large saucepan filled with 2 litres (3½ pints) of water. Bring the water to the boil and blanch the meat for 3 minutes. Drain the meat, transfer it to a plate, and set the plate aside.

Drain the chick-peas and return them to the heavy-bottomed saucepan. Pour in 1 litre (1¾ pints) of water and the stock, and bring to the boil over high heat. Add the blanched shanks and the salt, some pepper and the coriander. Reduce the heat to low and simmer the lamb and chick-peas for 45 minutes.

Add the onion, garlic, tomato paste, thyme and lemon juice to the lamb and chick-peas, and stir to combine them. Simmer the mixture until the lamb is very tender — 1 to 1½ hours.

Remove the meat from the pot and transfer it to a plate. Let it stand until it is cool enough to handle. Skim the fat from the surface of the chick-pea mixture and keep the mixture warm. Remove the meat from the shank bone and cut it into 1 cm (½ inch) pieces; discard the bone. Return the lamb pieces to the pot.

This dish can be served immediately or prepared a day in advance. To reheat, add 12.5 cl (4 fl oz) of water to the mixture, bring it to a simmer over a low heat and cook it for 10 minutes.

SUGGESTED ACCOMPANIMENT: *French bread; green salad.*

EDITOR'S NOTE: *You may have to ask your butcher in advance for the short shank end of leg required for this recipe.*

Scandinavian Casserole

SCANDINAVIANS TRADITIONALLY ENRICH THIS DILL-FLAVOURED STEW WITH EGGS AND CREAM. IN THE VERSION PRESENTED HERE, GREEK YOGURT ACHIEVES THE SAME SUMPTUOUS EFFECT WITH LESS CHOLESTEROL AND FAR FEWER CALORIES.

Serves 4
Working time: about 30 minutes
Total time: about 1 hour and 45 minutes

Calories **230**
Protein **30g**
Cholesterol **75mg**
Total fat **9g**
Saturated fat **3g**
Sodium **380mg**

500 g	lean lamb (from the leg or loin), trimmed of fat and cut into 2.5 cm (1 inch) cubes	1 lb
½ tsp	salt	½ tsp
1	small onion, quartered	1
2	fresh dill sprigs	2
1	bay leaf	1
4	black peppercorns	4
1	large bulb fennel (about 300 g/10 oz), trimmed and sliced vertically	1
125 g	button mushrooms, wiped and trimmed	4 oz
2 tsp	cornflour	2 tsp
1 tbsp	skimmed milk	1 tbsp
½	lemon, grated rind and juice	½
1 tsp	sugar	1 tsp
15 cl	thick Greek yogurt	¼ pint
1 tsp	mild German mustard	1 tsp
4 tbsp	chopped fresh dill	4 tbsp
¼ tsp	white pepper	¼ tsp

Place the lamb in a fireproof casserole and cover it with cold water; add ¼ teaspoon of the salt. Bring the water to the boil over medium heat and skim off the scum that rises to the surface. Add the onion, dill sprigs, bay leaf and peppercorns, then cover and simmer for 45 minutes.

Add the fennel to the casserole and simmer for a further 15 minutes. Stir in the mushrooms and continue simmering until the meat is very tender — about 15 minutes more. Lift the lamb, fennel and mushrooms out of the casserole with a slotted spoon and keep them warm while making the sauce.

Strain the stock through a fine sieve into a measuring jug. Rinse out the casserole and pour the strained stock back into it. The sauce requires 30 cl (½ pint) of stock: if you have more, then boil it rapidly to reduce it to that amount. Blend the cornflour with the milk and add it to the stock, stirring well. Cook the stock gently until it thickens — about 3 minutes. Stir the lemon rind and juice, and the sugar into the thickened stock.

Return the lamb and vegetables to the casserole and heat them gently, uncovered, for 5 minutes. Remove the casserole from the heat. Blend the yogurt with the mustard, chopped dill, white pepper and the remaining ¼ teaspoon of salt. Stir the seasoned yogurt into the casserole and serve immediately.

SUGGESTED ACCOMPANIMENT: *peas; baby carrots.*

Lamb Shanks with Orange and Cinnamon

Serves 4
Working time: about 45 minutes
Total time: about 2 hours and 40 minutes

Calories **285**			
Protein **20g**	4	lamb shanks (about 350 g/12 oz each), trimmed of fat	4
Cholesterol **50mg**	45 g	flour	1 ½ oz
Total fat **10g**		freshly ground black pepper	
Saturated fat **2g**	2 tbsp	chopped fresh oregano, or 2 tsp dried oregano	2 tbsp
Sodium **255mg**	1 ½ tbsp	safflower oil	1 ½ tbsp
	1	onion, chopped	1
	2	garlic cloves, finely chopped	2
	12.5 cl	red wine	4 fl oz
	4 tbsp	fresh orange juice	4 tbsp
	¼ tsp	salt	¼ tsp
	1	bay leaf	1
	1	cinnamon stick, or ¼ tsp ground cinnamon	1
	300 g	pearl onions, blanched for 2 minutes in boiling water and peeled	10 oz
	500 g	carrots, cut crosswise into 5 cm pieces	1 lb
	1 tbsp	julienned orange rind	1 tbsp
	4 tbsp	finely chopped parsley	4 tbsp

Put the flour, some pepper and half of the oregano into a large plastic bag. Add the shanks and shake the bag to coat the meat with the mixture.

Heat the oil in a large, heavy sauté pan over medium-high heat. Sauté the shanks, turning them from time to time, until they have browned. Add the chopped onion, reduce the heat and cover the pan. Cook for 5 minutes, stirring occasionally.

Increase the heat to medium high and add the garlic, wine, orange juice and ¾ litre (1 ¼ pints) of water. Bring the liquid to a simmer, scraping the bottom of the pan with a wooden spoon to dissolve any caramelized juices. Add the salt, bay leaf, cinnamon and the remaining oregano. Reduce the heat, cover the pan and continue simmering the meat until it is barely tender — 1½ to 2 hours.

Skim any fat from the surface of the liquid; add the pearl onions, carrots and orange rind. Simmer the lamb, partially covered, until the vegetables are tender — about 30 minutes.

Skim off any more fat, stir in the chopped parsley, and serve the lamb with the vegetables and the sauce.

SUGGESTED ACCOMPANIMENT: *basmati rice.*

EDITOR'S NOTE: *Shanks, the knuckle end of the hind leg or fore leg, may have to be ordered from the butcher in advance. If unavailable, use a 1.25 kg (2 ½ lb) leg of lamb, cut from the shank end, and prepare it in the same way.*

Braised Leg of Lamb with Mustard Seeds

Serves 8
Working time: about 40 minutes
Total time: about 3 hours

Calories **205**
Protein **20g**
Cholesterol **55mg**
Total fat **7g**
Saturated fat **2g**
Sodium **155mg**

1.5 kg	leg of lamb, shank end, trimmed of fat	3 lb
1 tbsp	virgin olive oil	1 tbsp
35 cl	stout	12 fl oz
¼ litre	unsalted brown stock (recipe, page 137)	8 fl oz
2	onions, quartered	2
3	garlic cloves	3
1 tsp	mustard seeds	1 tsp
½ tsp	celery seeds	½ tsp
¼ tsp	salt	¼ tsp
	freshly ground black pepper	
4	bay leaves	4
3	whole cloves	3
500 g	swede, peeled and cut into 2.5 cm (1 inch) cubes	1 lb
1 kg	green cabbage, quartered and cored, the leaves separated	2 lb

Heat the oil in a large, fireproof casserole set over high heat. When the oil is hot, add the lamb and brown it on all sides — about 10 minutes in all. Pour in the beer and the stock, then add the onions, garlic, mustard seeds, celery seeds, salt and some pepper. Tie up the bay leaves and cloves in a piece of muslin and add them to the casserole. Bring the liquid to the boil, then reduce the heat to maintain a simmer.

Cover the casserole, leaving the lid slightly ajar, and braise the lamb for about 1¼ hours, turning it two or three times during the cooking. Add the swede cubes and continue braising the lamb until it is tender — approximately 30 minutes more.

While the swede is cooking, pour enough water into a large pan to fill it about 2.5 cm (1 inch) deep. Set a vegetable steamer in the pan, add the cabbage, and cover the pan. Bring the water to the boil and steam the cabbage until it is tender — about 10 minutes.

Transfer the cabbage to a large platter and cover it loosely with aluminium foil. Remove the lamb from the casserole and set it on a carving board. With a slotted spoon, transfer the swede and onions to a bowl and cover them with foil too.

Remove the bundle of bay leaves and cloves from the casserole and discard it. Reduce the sauce over high heat until only about ¼ litre (8 fl oz) of it remains — about 10 minutes. Carve the lamb and arrange the slices on the cabbage. Surround the lamb with the swede and onions, then pour the sauce over the top. Serve at once.

SUGGESTED ACCOMPANIMENT: *wholemeal bread.*

Lamb Chili Verde

Serves 6
Working time: about 30 minutes
Total time: about 2 hours and 30 minutes (includes soaking)

Calories **360**
Protein **37g**
Cholesterol **75mg**
Total fat **12g**
Saturated fat **5g**
Sodium **185mg**

750 g	lean lamb (from the leg or loin), trimmed of fat and cut into 1 cm (½ inch) pieces	1 ½ lb
200 g	dried pinto beans, picked over	7 oz
1 tbsp	safflower oil	1 tbsp
1	onion, finely chopped	1
¼ tsp	salt	¼ tsp
	freshly ground black pepper	
2	garlic cloves, finely chopped	2
2	fresh hot green chili peppers, seeded and chopped (caution, box, right)	2
750 g	green tomatoes, skinned, seeded and coarsely chopped	1 ½ lb
35 cl	unsalted brown or chicken stock (recipes, page 137)	12 fl oz
2 tbsp	dark brown sugar	2 tbsp
½ tsp	cumin seeds	½ tsp
1	cucumber, peeled, seeded and coarsely chopped	1
30 g	Cheddar cheese, grated	1 oz

Rinse the pinto beans under cold running water, then put them into a large, heavy-bottomed saucepan and pour in enough water to cover them by about 7.5 cm (3 inches). Discard any beans that float to the surface. Cover the pan, leaving the lid ajar, and slowly bring the liquid to the boil over medium-low heat. Boil the beans for 2 minutes, then turn off the heat and soak the beans, covered, for at least 1 hour. (Alternatively, soak the beans in cold water overnight.)

Heat the oil in a large, heavy-bottomed saucepan over medium-high heat. Add the lamb pieces and sauté them until they are browned on all sides — about 3 minutes. Reduce the heat to medium and add the onion, the salt and some pepper. Cook the mixture, stirring frequently, until the onion is translucent — about 3 minutes. Add the garlic and cook the mixture for 1 minute more. Drain the beans and add them to the pan. Stir in the chili peppers, all but 125 g (4 oz) of the tomatoes, the stock, brown sugar, cumin seeds and ½ litre (16 fl oz) of water. Bring the mixture to a simmer and cook it, covered, for 1 hour. Add the cucumber and remaining tomatoes and simmer for a further 15 minutes, then remove the lid and continue simmering the chili until the beans are tender — approximately 15 minutes more.

Ladle the chili into six individual bowls and top it with the grated cheese.

SUGGESTED ACCOMPANIMENTS: *sweetcorn salad; crusty white bread.*

Chili Peppers — a Cautionary Note

Both dried and fresh hot chili peppers should be handled with care. Their flesh and seeds contain volatile oils that can make skin tingle and cause eyes to burn. Rubber gloves offer protection — but the cook should still be careful not to touch the face, lips or eyes when working with chilies.

Soaking fresh chilies in cold, salted water for an hour will remove some of their fire. If canned chilies are substituted for fresh ones, they should be rinsed in cold water in order to eliminate as much of the brine used to preserve them as possible.

Red Pepper and Okra Lamb Stew

Serves 4
Working time: about 20 minutes
Total time: about 1 hour

Calories **380**
Protein **35g**
Cholesterol **90mg**
Total fat **13g**
Saturated fat **4g**
Sodium **125mg**

600 g	lean lamb (from the leg or loin), trimmed of fat and cut into 2.5 cm (1 inch) pieces	1 ¼ lb
2 tbsp	plain flour	2 tbsp
2 tbsp	paprika	2 tbsp
⅛ tsp	salt	⅛ tsp
	freshly ground black pepper	
1 tbsp	safflower oil	1 tbsp
1	onion, finely chopped	1
35 cl	unsalted brown or chicken stock (recipes, page 137)	12 fl oz
2 tsp	cider vinegar	2 tsp
1 tsp	Dijon mustard	1 tsp
8 drops	Tabasco sauce	8 drops
1	garlic clove, finely chopped	1
1	sweet red pepper, seeded, deribbed and cut into 2.5 cm (1 inch) strips	1
250 g	okra, trimmed, sliced diagonally into 2 cm (¾ inch) pieces	8 oz

Combine the flour and paprika in a large bowl. Season the lamb pieces with the salt and some freshly ground black pepper, then toss them in the flour mixture. Remove the meat from the bowl, shaking off any excess flour, and set it aside.

Heat 2 teaspoons of the oil in a fireproof casserole over medium-high heat. Add the lamb pieces and chopped onion, and cook them, stirring continuously, until the onion is translucent and the meat is browned — 2 to 3 minutes. Stir in the stock, cider vinegar, mustard, Tasbaco sauce and chopped garlic, and bring the mixture to a simmer. Continue to simmer the stew for 30 minutes.

Heat the remaining teaspoon of oil in a non-stick frying pan over medium-high heat and stir-fry the sweet pepper strips and the sliced okra for 2 minutes. Then transfer the vegetables to the casserole containing the lamb and simmer the stew until the meat is tender — 20 to 30 minutes.

SUGGESTED ACCOMPANIMENT: *boiled rice.*

Lamb Poached in Buttermilk

Serves 4
Working time: about 15 minutes
Total time: about 1 hour and 15 minutes

Calories **480**
Protein **34g**
Cholesterol **80mg**
Total fat **13g**
Saturated fat **3g**
Sodium **410mg**

600 g	lean lamb (from the leg or loin), trimmed of fat and cut into 2 cm (¾ inch) cubes	1¼ lb
2 tsp	safflower oil	2 tsp
1	sweet green pepper, seeded, deribbed and cut into 2.5 cm (1 inch) squares	1
1	onion, cut into 2.5 cm (1 inch) cubes	1
¼ tsp	salt	¼ tsp
	white pepper	
1	large carrot, cut into 2.5 cm (1 inch) pieces	1
2 tsp	caraway seeds	2 tsp
	cayenne pepper	
35 cl	unsalted chicken stock (recipe, page 137)	12 fl oz
¼ litre	buttermilk	8 fl oz
1½ tbsp	cornflour	1½ tbsp
250 g	dried egg noodles	8 oz

Heat the oil in a large heavy-bottomed saucepan set over medium heat. Add the green pepper squares and onion cubes, and cook them, stirring frequently, until the onion is translucent — about 5 minutes. Add the lamb, salt, some white pepper, the carrot, caraway seeds, a pinch of cayenne pepper and the chicken stock; bring the liquid to a simmer. Mix the buttermilk and cornflour in a small bowl, then whisk them into the simmering liquid. Cover the saucepan, leaving the lid slightly ajar, and simmer the lamb until it is tender — about 45 minutes.

Add the noodles to 3 litres (5 pints) of boiling water with 1½ teaspoons of salt. Start testing the noodles after 6 minutes and cook them until they are al dente. Drain the noodles and transfer them to a serving dish. Top the noodles with the lamb and serve at once.

SUGGESTED ACCOMPANIMENT: *steamed kale or spring greens.*

Mongolian Hot Pot

CENTRAL TO THIS ANCIENT ORIENTAL DISH IS THE
"FIREPOT" OF BOILING BROTH, WHICH FIRST COOKS THE MEAT
AND VEGETABLES AT THE TABLE AND THEN PROVIDES A
NOURISHING SOUP.

Serves 4
Working time: about 1 hour
Total time: about 7 hours (includes chilling)

Calories **385**
Protein **38g**
Cholesterol **75mg**
Total fat **12g**
Saturated fat **4g**
Sodium **100mg**

500 g	lean lamb (from the loin), trimmed of fat	1 lb
300 g	firm tofu (bean curd), cut into strips about 4 by 1 cm (1½ by ½ inch)	10 oz
250 g	button mushrooms, wiped and trimmed	8 oz
250 g	mange-tout, stems and strings removed	8 oz
250 g	sweet red pepper, seeded, deribbed and cut into thin strips	8 oz
200 g	Chinese cabbage, shredded	7 oz
150 g	spinach leaves, stems removed, washed	5 oz
3	spring onions, trimmed and finely chopped	3
2	garlic cloves, peeled and crushed	2
1 cm	piece fresh ginger root, peeled and finely chopped	½ inch
2 tbsp	chopped fresh coriander	2 tbsp
125 g	rice noodles, broken into short lengths	4 oz
Chicken and ginger broth		
750 g	small pieces of chicken on the bone, skin removed, trimmed of fat	1½ lb
5 cm	piece fresh ginger root, roughly chopped	2 inch
3	spring onions, cut in half	3
6	fresh coriander sprigs	6
30 cl	rice wine or dry sherry	1 fl oz
Dipping sauce		
6 tbsp	low-sodium soy sauce or shoyu	6 tbsp
1½ tsp	muscovado sugar	1½ tsp
3	spring onions, trimmed and finely chopped	3
2 cm	piece fresh ginger root, finely chopped	¾ inch
2	garlic cloves, crushed	2
	Tabasco sauce	

Prepare the broth at least 7 hours in advance. Put the chicken in a large saucepan with the ginger, spring onions and coriander. Pour in 2 litres (3½ pints) of cold water, bring it to the boil, then skim off the scum with a slotted spoon. Reduce the heat, cover and simmer gently for 2 hours. Remove the cooked chicken and

reserve for use in another recipe. Strain the broth into a bowl, leave it to cool, then chill it in the refrigerator for at least 4 hours, or overnight, until any fat forms a solid layer on the surface.

About 1 hour before serving, wrap the lamb in foil and place it in the freezer until it is semi-frozen. Meanwhile, make the dipping sauce. In a bowl, whisk together all the ingredients except the Tabasco sauce and set aside.

Lift off and discard the surface fat on the chilled chicken broth, then heat the broth gently in a saucepan until it liquefies. Stir the rice wine or sherry into the broth. Dilute the dipping sauce with 4 tablespoons of the broth and add drops of Tabasco sauce to taste. Divide the sauce equally among four individual bowls.

Unwrap the lamb and cut it across the grain into paper-thin slices with a very sharp knife. Arrange the lamb, tofu, mushrooms, mange-tout, red pepper, Chinese cabbage and spinach on a large platter. Lay chopsticks, a bowl of dipping sauce and a soup bowl and soup spoon at each place setting.

Stir the spring onions, garlic, ginger and coriander into the broth and bring it to the boil. Fill a prepared firepot or metal fondue pot with boiling broth and place the pot in the centre of the table. As the meal progresses, cook the lamb, tofu and vegetables in the broth, allowing 30 seconds to 1 minute according to taste. Scoop out each batch of cooked food with a wire mesh spoon and distribute it among the diners' soup bowls, to be dipped into the sauce and eaten. When all the lamb, tofu and vegetables have been consumed, bring any remaining broth to the boil, pour it back into the pot, and stir in the noodles. Cook them for 2 to 3 minutes to soften them, then ladle the broth and noodles into the soup bowls.

EDITORS NOTE: *Firepots, heated by charcoal, are available from Oriental food shops; they come complete with wire mesh spoons for lifting the ingredients out of the hot stock. A metal fondue set makes a perfect substitute.*

3 *A herb sauce cloaks pancakes filled with a savoury sauté of minced lamb, onion and mushroom (recipe, page 100); the ensemble will heat through in the oven.*

Inspired Combinations

The many ways of preparing lamb do not end with simple dry or moist cooking. Lamb can be part of a salad, a stuffing or a pie. It can be moulded in aspic or wrapped in green leaves. This chapter explores a number of imaginative presentations using lamb in dishes of this kind, devised or adapted for the health-conscious cook.

Lamb and vegetables combine to form a naturally happy marriage. Vegetables that are suitable for stuffing range from less-known varieties such as acorn squash *(page 118)*, to the more homely potato *(page 114)* and onion *(page 115)*. Baked assemblies of lamb and sliced vegetables include not only the moussaka on page 109, but also unusual combinations such as the loin chops layered with fennel, potatoes and courgettes on page 110.

Enclosing lamb in pasta or pastry is the basis for a number of other ideas. One of the most successful wrapping materials is phyllo pastry — a low-fat, paper-thin dough that provides the crispness of a pastry crust with only a fraction of the calories that are found in shortcrust or puff dough.

As befits a universally esteemed meat, many of the recipes have an exotic flavour. Marinated in the traditional ''five-spice'' seasoning of China, a leg of lamb acquires a distinctive Oriental appeal *(page 120)*. Sautéed with chili peppers and tomatoes, diced lamb and beans fill a Mexican tortilla *(page 101)*. A Salade Niçoise using roast lamb *(page 90)* and a lasagne layered with lamb and sweet peppers *(page 102)* draw on Mediterranean traditions.

Whether mixed with plum purée in a stuffing for Mongolian dumplings *(page 103)*, or rolled up with mushrooms in pancakes *(left)*, minced lamb plays an important part in many of the recipes. Ready-minced lamb is rare and, when available, is invariably fatty. In addition, butchers are not always willing to mince lean meat in the small quantities required; but mincing by hand, as shown on page 43, is a straightforward technique. By purchasing lean lamb, then trimming it of all excess fat and mincing it yourself, you can be assured of a high-quality mince.

Salade Niçoise

Serves 6
Working time: about 50 minutes
Total time: about 1 hour and 15 minutes

Calories **330**
Protein **31g**
Cholesterol **75mg**
Total fat **14g**
Saturated fat **6g**
Sodium **270mg**

1 kg	loin of lamb, trimmed of fat	2¼ lb
	freshly ground black pepper	
500 g	small new potatoes, scrubbed	1 lb
250 g	French beans, topped and tailed	8 oz
½	cucumber	½
3	tomatoes, cut into thin wedges	3
1	round lettuce, washed and dried	1
3	anchovy fillets, rinsed, patted dry with paper towels and chopped	3
6	black olives, stoned and halved	6
Herb vinaigrette		
2	garlic cloves, crushed	2
1 tsp	Dijon mustard	1 tsp
¼ tsp	salt	¼ tsp
3 tbsp	fresh lemon juice	3 tbsp
1 tbsp	virgin olive oil	1 tbsp
1 tbsp	chopped parsley	1 tbsp
1 tbsp	chopped fresh basil	1 tbsp
½ tbsp	chopped fresh oregano	½ tbsp

Preheat the oven to 230°C (450°F or Mark 8). Season the loin all over with black pepper, place it in a roasting pan and cook it for 45 minutes to 1 hour for rare to medium meat. Allow it to cool at room temperature while preparing the vegetables.

Boil the potatoes until they are tender — 20 to 25 minutes — then drain them and let them cool. Cook the beans in boiling water until they are tender but still crisp — 3 to 4 minutes. Drain them and rinse them under cold running water.

Peel the cucumber and cut it in half lengthwise. Scoop out the seeds and discard them, then cut each half into slices.

To make the vinaigrette, mix together the garlic, mustard and salt in a small bowl, then whisk in the lemon juice and olive oil. Stir in the chopped parsley, basil and oregano, and set aside.

Cut the loin off the bone and cut the meat into strips about 7.5 cm (3 inches) long by 1 cm (½ inch) wide. Put the strips of meat into a large bowl, add the vinaigrette and stir to thoroughly coat them. Add the potatoes, French beans, cucumber and tomatoes and toss all the ingredients together.

Line a salad bowl with the lettuce leaves and transfer the tossed salad into it. Sprinkle the salad with the chopped anchovies and add the olives.

SUGGESTED ACCOMPANIMENT: *herbed garlic bread.*

EDITOR'S NOTE: *This recipe is a good way of using lean, left-over roast lamb.*

Roast Lamb and Pink Grapefruit Salad

Serves 8
Working time: about 35 minutes
Total time: about 2 hours and 50 minutes (includes cooling)

Calories **265**
Protein **30g**
Cholesterol **75mg**
Total fat **14g**
Saturated fat **6g**
Sodium **170mg**

2 kg	leg of lamb, trimmed of fat	4 lb
2	pink grapefruits	2
1 tbsp	safflower oil	1 tbsp
1 tbsp	Dijon mustard	1 tbsp
1 tbsp	dry mustard	1 tbsp
1 tbsp	clear honey	1 tbsp
	freshly ground black pepper	
400 g	mixed salad leaves, such as oakleaf, red lollo and watercress	14 oz
Mustard-honey dressing		
1 tsp	Dijon mustard	1 tsp
½ tsp	dry mustard	½ tsp
1 tsp	clear honey	1 tsp
½ tsp	salt	½ tsp
¼ tsp	white pepper	¼ tsp
1 tsp	wine vinegar	1 tsp
1 tbsp	safflower oil	1 tbsp
1 tbsp	hazelnut oil	1 tbsp

Preheat the oven to 230°C (450°F or Mark 8). Finely grate the rind of one grapefruit into a small mixing bowl. Add the safflower oil, Dijon mustard, dry mustard and honey. Mix them well and spread the mustafld paste all over the lamb. Season generously with black pepper.

Put the lamb in a roasting pan and cook it for 15 minutes. Reduce the heat to 180°C (350°F or Mark 4) and continue to roast the lamb until it is cooked — 1 hour to 1¼ hours for rare to medium-rare meat. Then rest the lamb at room temperature for at least 1 hour; if you are serving it much later in the day, chill it as soon as it has cooled to room temperature.

Remove the skin and white pith from both grapefruits. Holding each grapefruit over a bowl to catch the juice, carefully remove the segments by cutting between the flesh and the connecting membrane with a sharp knife. Keep the segments separate from the juice.

To make the dressing, whisk together the mustards, honey, salt, white pepper and wine vinegar. Whisk in the oils, and finally 4 tablespoons of the grapefruit juice. Toss the salad leaves in the dressing. Carve the meat and serve the slices alternated with the grapefruit segments, accompanied by the salad leaves.

SUGGESTED ACCOMPANIMENT: *French bread.*

Gyros

TRADITIONAL FARE IN GREEK HOMES, GYROS IS MADE UP OF
LAYERS OF MEAT AND HERBS AND COOKED ON A BARBECUE.
THE ACCOMPANYING TZATZIKI IS A YOGURT SAUCE SEASONED
WITH CUCUMBER AND DILL.

Serves 12
Working time: about 45 minutes
Total time: about 2 hours (includes marinating)

Calories **360**
Protein **35g**
Cholesterol **80mg**
Total fat **10g**
Saturated fat **3g**
Sodium **330mg**

1.25 kg	boneless leg of lamb, trimmed of fat	2 ½ lb
500 g	beef rump steak, trimmed of fat	1 lb
1	lemon, juice only	1
3	garlic cloves, finely chopped	3
3 tbsp	finely chopped fresh oregano, or 1 tbsp dried oregano	3 tbsp
½ tsp	ground coriander	½ tsp
½ tsp	salt	½ tsp
	freshly ground black pepper	
2	egg whites	2
½ tbsp	paprika	½ tbsp
1 tbsp	safflower oil	1 tbsp
12	pitta breads, cut in half	12
1	cos lettuce, washed, dried and shredded	1
3	large ripe tomatoes, chopped	3

Tzatziki		
¼ litre	plain low-fat yogurt	8 fl oz
1	cucumber, peeled, halved and seeded	1
4 tbsp	finely cut fresh dill, or 3 tbsp chopped parsley mixed with 1 tbsp dried dill	4 tbsp
½ tsp	distilled white vinegar	½ tsp
⅛ tsp	salt	⅛ tsp

Cut the lamb against the grain into thin slices. Place the lamb slices between two sheets of plastic film or greaseproof paper, and pound the meat with a meat bat or the flat of a heavy knife *(page 24)* to a thickness of about 3 mm (⅛ inch). Transfer the slices to a bowl.

Cut the beef against the grain into slices about 5 mm (¼ inch) thick. Pound the slices as you did the lamb and transfer them to a second bowl.

In a small bowl, stir together the lemon juice, garlic, oregano, coriander, salt and some pepper. Divide this mixture between the beef and lamb slices, and toss them in their separate bowls to distribute the seasonings evenly. In another small bowl, lightly beat the egg whites with the paprika.

To assemble the gyros, brush a slice of beef with some of the egg white mixture and set the slice on a clean work surface. Top the beef with two slices of lamb and brush them with egg white mixture, too. Continue stacking and brushing the beef and lamb slices, ending with a slice of beef. Press down on the stack to compact it, forcing out any excess liquid. Insert a long metal skewer through the stack, slightly off centre, then lay the stack on its side and thread a second skewer through the meat from the other end. Let the gyros stand at room temperature for 1 to 2 hours before cooking it.

To make the tzatziki, purée the yogurt, cucumber, dill, vinegar and salt in a food processor or a blender. Transfer the sauce to a bowl and chill it.

About 30 minutes before cooking time, light the charcoal in the barbecue. When the coals are hot, bank them against the sides of the barbecue. Place a foil drip pan in the centre of the grate and set the rack in place. Brush the gyros with the oil and lay it on the centre of the rack. Cook the gyros, turning it often to ensure that it cooks evenly — about 30 minutes for medium-cooked meat.

Remove the gyros from the rack and let it rest for 10 minutes before removing the skewers. With a very sharp knife, cut the meat lengthwise into thin slices. Fill the pitta pockets with the meat, lettuce, tomato and tzatziki sauce. Serve immediately.

SUGGESTED ACCOMPANIMENT: *pickled chili peppers.*

Warm Mediterranean Lamb Salad

Serves 4
Working time: about 35 minutes
Total time: about 2 hours and 15 minutes

Calories **280**
Protein **32g**
Cholesterol **95mg**
Total fat **13g**
Saturated fat **5g**
Sodium **350mg**

1.25 kg	leg of lamb, shank end, trimmed of fat	2½ lb
¼ tsp	salt	¼ tsp
	freshly ground black pepper	
1 tbsp	virgin olive oil	1 tbsp
2	onions, thinly sliced	2
2	garlic cloves, finely chopped	2
2 tsp	fresh thyme, or ½ tsp dried thyme	2 tsp
¾ tsp	dry mustard	¾ tsp
7.5 cl	cider vinegar	2½ fl oz
1	Batavian endive, trimmed, washed, dried and cut crosswise into 2.5 cm (1 inch) wide strips	1
2	ripe tomatoes, cored and cut into thin wedges	2
45 g	feta cheese	1½ oz

Preheat the oven to 180°C (350°F or Mark 4). Sprinkle the lamb with the salt and a generous grinding of pep-per. Place it in a heavy roasting pan and roast it until it is tender — 1½ to 2 hours — turning it once after 1 hour and adding 2 or 3 tablespoons of water if the juices begin to burn. Remove the lamb from the oven and set it aside to cool; do not wash the roasting pan.

When the meat is cool enough to handle, pull it off the bone and tear it into shreds with your fingers. Transfer the meat to a bowl, cover it loosely with aluminium foil, and keep it warm.

Spoon off any fat that has accumulated in the roast-ing pan and set the pan over medium-low heat. Stir in the oil, onions, garlic, thyme, mustard and a generous grinding of pepper. Cook the mixture, scraping up the caramelized juices with a wooden spoon, until the onions are translucent — 10 to 15 minutes. Pour in the vinegar and continue cooking the mixture, stirring con-stantly, for 1 minute. Add the endive and the tomato wedges, and keep stirring the salad until the endive begins to wilt — about 1 minute. Stir in the shredded lamb and toss well.

Transfer the tossed salad to a serving bowl. Then crumble the feta cheese on top and serve the salad while it is still warm.

SUGGESTED ACCOMPANIMENT: *French bread.*

EDITOR'S NOTE: *You may have to ask your butcher in advance for the short shank end of the leg required for this recipe.*

Aspic Mould with Summer Vegetables

TO MAKE A CLEAR VEGETABLE ASPIC, THE BOWLS AND COOKING UTENSILS MUST BE SCRUPULOUSLY CLEAN. HERE, EVERYTHING IS SCALDED TO ENSURE THAT THE LIQUID DOES NOT BECOME CLOUDED BY IMPURITIES.

Serves 6
Working time: about 2 hours
Total time: about 15 hours and 30 minutes
(includes chilling and setting)

Calories **320**
Protein **33g**
Cholesterol **75mg**
Total fat **12g**
Saturated fat **3g**
Sodium **270mg**

1 kg	lean lamb on the bone, cut from the fillet end of the leg	2 lb
1 ½ tsp	salt	1 ½ tsp
1	leek, white part only, sliced and washed	1
1	small onion, sliced	1
1	carrot, sliced	1
1	parsnip, sliced	1
1	bay leaf	1
2	parsley sprigs	2
8	black peppercorns	8
100 g	very small new carrots, trimmed	3 ½ oz
100 g	young French beans, topped and tailed	3 ½ oz
125 g	powdered gelatine	4 oz
4	eggs, whites and shells only	4
4 tbsp	Madeira	4 tbsp
1 tbsp	fresh chervil fronds	1 tbsp
1 tbsp	capers, rinsed	1 tbsp
	curly endive or lettuce, for garnish	

Place the lamb in a large non-reactive saucepan and cover it with cold water. Bring the water to the boil, then reduce the heat and simmer the lamb for 3 minutes. Transfer the lamb to a colander standing in the sink, drain off the water and rinse the lamb with a kettleful of boiling water. Rinse the saucepan.

Return the lamb to the saucepan and add the salt, leek, onion, carrot, parsnip, bay leaf, parsley and black peppercorns. Pour in just enough cold water to cover the lamb and the vegetables. Bring the liquid to the boil over moderate heat, skimming off any scum that rises to the surface. Partially cover the saucepan, reduce the heat to low and simmer the lamb until a thin skewer inserted in the centre of the meat easily penetrates to the bone — 2 to 2½ hours. Remove the saucepan from the heat. Allow the lamb to cool in the liquid to room temperature — 1½ to 2 hours — then

refrigerate it for at least 6 hours or overnight.

Remove and discard the layer of fat from the surface of the chilled stock, together with any pieces of fat adhering to the lamb. Strain the stock into a clean bowl; discard the vegetables.

Cook the small whole carrots in a little of the skimmed stock until they are tender — about 10 minutes — then remove them with a slotted spoon and set them aside. Cook the French beans in the same stock for about 5 minutes; remove them and set them aside. Return the stock to the bowl.

Put a large piece of muslin, a wire balloon whisk and a large metal sieve into a large saucepan. Fill the saucepan with cold water and bring it to the boil to scald the contents and the saucepan. Pour the boiling water into a large mixing bowl, to scald that also, then pour the water away. Wring out the muslin. Line the sieve with the muslin and place it over the mixing bowl.

Measure the stock; you should have about 1.75 litres (3 pints). If not, make up the quantity with chicken stock or water. Pour the stock into the scalded saucepan, then add the gelatine, egg whites, egg shells and Madeira. Place the saucepan over medium heat and bring the mixture to the boil, whisking with the balloon whisk until a thick foam forms on the surface. Stop whisking and allow the liquid to boil until the foam rises to the top of the saucepan. At once remove the saucepan from the heat and allow the foam to settle back down in the saucepan. Repeat this process twice more, without whisking, then remove the saucepan from the heat and allow it to stand for 10 minutes. Carefully pour the liquid into the muslin-lined sieve, without allowing the foam to break up. When the liquid has completely drained through the muslin, discard the foam. Allow the strained aspic jelly to stand until it is cool but not set — about 1 hour.

Meanwhile, prepare the lamb. Cut the meat from the bone, following muscle divisions where possible. Remove any remaining fat and tendons. Slice each piece of meat across the grain into thin medallions, about 1 cm (½ inch) thick and 5 cm (2 inches) long.

Pour a thin layer of the cold aspic into the bottom of a 1.5 litre (2½ pint) rectangular loaf tin. Refrigerate until the aspic sets — about 5 minutes. Remove the tin from the refrigerator. Dip the chervil fronds in the liquid aspic, then arrange them decoratively over the set aspic. Refrigerate the tin for 2 to 3 minutes to set the fronds in position, then pour in just enough aspic to cover them. Refrigerate for a further 5 minutes.

Select one third of the most attractive, even-sized, medallions of lamb and arrange them neatly over the set aspic in the mould. Pour in just enough aspic to cover the lamb, then refrigerate the tin for 10 minutes.

Arrange the carrots and the capers over the lamb. Cover them with a little more aspic and refrigerate the tin for 10 minutes to set. Continue building up the mould with two more layers: half of the remaining lamb topped with the beans. Cover each layer with a little of the aspic and chill it for 10 minutes before proceeding. Finally, arrange the remaining lamb over the set beans and cover it with the remaining aspic. Refrigerate the mould until it is very firmly set — at least 4 hours.

To unmould the aspic, loosen the top edges carefully with a thin-bladed knife and invert the mould on to a flat serving dish. Soak a tea towel in very hot water, wring it out and wrap it round the outside of the mould. Repeat the soaking and wrapping until you can lift the tin off, after freeing the mould with a gentle shake. Garnish with a few lettuce leaves.

SUGGESTED ACCOMPANIMENT: *potato salad; mixed lettuce salad.*

EDITOR'S NOTE: *Any remaining aspic can be allowed to set, and then chopped for garnish round the mould. Aspic may be made up to two or three days in advance and kept in the refrigerator until needed. Once set, it can be quickly melted by placing the bowl over a saucepan of hot water.*

Phyllo-Wrapped Cutlets with Quince

Serves 8
Working time: about 1 hour and 15 minutes
Total time: about 2 hours

Calories **240**			
Protein **14g**	8	best end of neck cutlets (about 90 g/3 oz each), trimmed of fat	8
Cholesterol **60mg**		freshly ground black pepper	
Total fat **11g**	200 g	fresh chestnuts, shelled and peeled	7 oz
Saturated fat **5g**	30 cl	unsalted brown or chicken stock (recipes, page 137)	½ pint
Sodium **185mg**	1	cinnamon stick	1
	¾ tsp	salt	¾ tsp
	300 g	fresh quinces	10 oz
	1 tbsp	sugar	1 tbsp
	1 tsp	fresh lemon juice	1 tsp
	2 tbsp	quince preserve	2 tbsp
	1 tbsp	clear honey	1 tbsp
	1 tsp	ground cinnamon	1 tsp
	30 g	unsalted butter	1 oz
	1 tbsp	virgin olive oil	1 tbsp
	16	sheets phyllo pastry, each 30 by 17.5 cm (12 by 7 inches)	16

Sprinkle the cutlets generously with black pepper and leave them at room temperature while you prepare the chestnuts and quinces.

Put the chestnuts in a saucepan with the stock and half the cinnamon stick. Cover the pan, bring the stock to the boil and boil until the chestnuts are tender — 20 to 30 minutes — topping up with water if necessary. Remove the cooked chestnuts, discard the cinnamon and rapidly boil the remaining stock until only about 4 tablespoons of liquid remain. Press the chestnuts through a sieve or grind them to fine crumbs in a food processor, then stir in enough of the reduced stock to make a thick purée. Season the purée with ¼ teaspoon of the salt and set it aside to cool.

Peel, quarter and core the quinces, retaining the trimmings. Cut the flesh lengthwise into 5 mm (¼ inch) thick slices. Put the fruit and trimmings into a non-reactive saucepan together with the sugar, lemon juice and remaining half stick of cinnamon. Cover with water and simmer over low heat until the quinces are completely tender — 10 to 30 minutes. Lift out the pieces of cooked fruit and put them on a plate; discard the trimmings and cooking liquid. Finely dice any pieces of fruit in the quince preserve, then gently warm the preserve and spoon it over the slices of quince. Set the glazed quince aside.

Preheat the grill to high. Lightly brush the grill pan with olive oil, then arrange the cutlets in the pan and spread half of the honey over their upper surfaces. Grill them until the honey begins to caramelize — about 1 minute — then turn them, spread the remaining honey over the uncooked sides and grill them for a further 1 minute. Set the cutlets aside for 10 minutes to cool. Meanwhile, preheat the oven to 190°C (375°F or Mark 5), and lightly oil a baking sheet. Season the cutlets on both sides with the remaining salt and some pepper. Spread the chestnut purée on top of the cutlets and cover them with the slices of quince. Sprinkle the prepared cutlets with the cinnamon.

In a small pan, melt the butter with the olive oil over low heat. Take one sheet of phyllo pastry and lay it out flat on a work surface with a short side nearest to you. Brush it with a little of the butter mixture, then place another sheet on top. Cover the remaining sheets of phyllo with a damp cloth or plastic film to prevent them from becoming brittle.

Position one of the cutlets on the doubled sheet of pastry, angling it so that the rib bone protrudes 2.5 cm (1 inch) beyond the lower left-hand corner. Fold the lower right-hand corner of the pastry over the cutlet, then fold over the right-hand side of the pastry, partially covering the cutlet. Carefully roll the cutlet up in the pastry to enclose it completely. Trim off any excess pastry to ensure the seams are underneath. Pinch the pastry tightly round the bone. Wrap the remaining cutlets in the same way. Place them seam side down on the baking sheet. Brush the pastry with the remaining oil and butter mixture, and bake the cutlets until they are golden-brown — 12 to 15 minutes. Allow them to rest at room temperature for 5 minutes before serving.

SUGGESTED ACCOMPANIMENT: *French beans.*

EDITOR'S NOTE: *To shell and peel chestnuts slit the shells down the rounded side and parboil them for 1 to 2 minutes. Remove the shell and peel while the chestnuts are still hot.*

Lamb and Courgette Pie

Serves 6
Working time: about 1 hour
Total time: about 2 hours and 25 minutes

Calories **240**
Protein **21g**
Cholesterol **75mg**
Total fat **12g**
Saturated fat **4g**
Sodium **220mg**

500 g	lean lamb (from the fillet end of the leg), trimmed of fat and cut into 5 mm (¼ inch) dice	1 lb
1 tbsp	virgin olive oil	1 tbsp
1	large onion, finely chopped	1
2	garlic cloves, crushed	2
250 g	carrots, cut into 5 mm (¼ inch) dice	8 oz
250 g	courgettes, cut into 5 mm (¼ inch) dice	8 oz
30 g	plain flour	1 oz
¼ litre	unsalted brown or chicken stock (recipes, page 137)	8 fl oz
1 tsp	mixed dried herbs	1 tsp
½ tsp	salt	½ tsp
	freshly ground black pepper	
5	sheets phyllo pastry, each 45 by 30 cm (18 by 12 inches)	5
30 g	polyunsaturated margarine, melted	1 oz

Heat the oil in a large, heavy sauté pan over medium heat. Add the onion, garlic and carrots. Reduce the heat to low and cook gently until the vegetables are soft but not brown — 10 to 15 minutes. Increase the heat to high, then add the diced lamb. Stir with a wooden spoon to keep the pieces of meat separated, until the lamb changes colour — 1 to 2 minutes. Add the courgettes, then stir in the flour, stock, mixed herbs, salt and pepper to taste. Bring the liquid to the boil, stirring. Reduce the heat to low, cover the pan and simmer until the courgettes are soft — 8 to 10 minutes. Remove the pan from the heat and allow the lamb mixture to cool for about 45 minutes.

Preheat the oven to 220°C (425°F or Mark 7). Pour the lamb mixture into a 20 cm (8 inch) pie plate.

Cut four of the phyllo sheets in half widthwise. Brush the edge of the pie plate with a little cold water, then cover the meat mixture with one of the half phyllo sheets, brush the phyllo with a little of the melted margarine and cover it with another sheet of phyllo. Repeat with the remaining six half sheets of phyllo. Using scissors, cut the pastry to fit the dish exactly.

Fold the remaining sheet of phyllo into four, trim the edges, then cut it lengthwise into two strips and cut these into diamond shapes. Brush the top of the pie with the melted margarine, then decorate it with the phyllo diamond shapes, brushing them individually with the margarine so that they stay in place. Make a small hole in the centre of the pie to allow the steam to escape during cooking.

Place the pie on a baking sheet and cook it in the oven until the pastry is golden-brown — 35 to 40 minutes. Serve immediately.

SUGGESTED ACCOMPANIMENTS: *green salad; steamed new potatoes tossed in parsley.*

Spinach and Lamb Strudel

Serves 4
Working time: about 30 minutes
Total time: about 1 hour and 15 minutes

Calories **200**
Protein **23g**
Cholesterol **70mg**
Total fat **7g**
Saturated fat **3g**
Sodium **235mg**

300 g	lean lamb (from the leg or loin), trimmed of fat and finely diced	10 oz
250 g	fresh spinach, washed and stemmed	8 oz
250 g	button mushrooms, finely chopped	8 oz
1	onion, finely chopped	1
30 g	wholemeal breadcrumbs	1 oz
2	garlic cloves, crushed	2
¼ tsp	salt	¼ tsp
	freshly ground black pepper	
2	sheets phyllo pastry, each 45 by 30 cm (18 by 12 inches)	2
½ tsp	safflower oil	½ tsp
1 tsp	sesame seeds	1 tsp
	cherry tomatoes, for garnish	

Preheat the oven to 190°C (375°F or Mark 5).

Set aside four spinach leaves for garnish then plunge the rest into a saucepan of boiling water, bring it back to the boil and cook for 1 minute. Drain it in a colander and rinse under cold water, then squeeze it dry and chop it finely.

Brush a non-stick frying pan with oil, heat it over a high heat then sear the lamb quickly. Remove the pan from the heat and stir in the spinach, mushrooms, onion, breadcrumbs, garlic, salt and pepper. Mix all the ingredients thoroughly together.

Lay one sheet of the phyllo on a work surface and cover it with the second sheet. Spoon the lamb filling along one short side of the phyllo, keeping it 2.5 cm (1 inch) away from the edge. Shape the filling into a firm sausage with your fingers. Roll up the strudel and transfer it to a baking sheet, seam side down. Squeeze the ends of the phyllo together lightly to stop the filling falling out. Brush the strudel with the oil and sprinkle it with the sesame seeds. Bake it until the pastry is golden — about 40 minutes. Leave it to cool for about 5 minutes before cutting it into eight slices. Serve the strudel garnished with the reserved spinach leaves and cherry tomatoes.

SUGGESTED ACCOMPANIMENT: *tomato and basil salad.*

Phyllo-Wrapped Lamb Medallions

A MEDALLION IS A SMALL OVAL OR ROUND SLICE OF MEAT.

Serves 4
Working time: about 25 minutes
Total time: about 45 minutes

Calories **325**			
Protein **28g**	1 kg	loin, boned and trimmed of fat, eye only (page 134)	2¼ lb
Cholesterol **80mg**	1	ripe pear	1
Total fat **12g**	2 tsp	safflower oil	2 tsp
Saturated fat **4g**	¼ tsp	salt	¼ tsp
Sodium **320mg**		freshly ground black pepper	
	2 tsp	finely chopped fresh ginger root	2 tsp
	12.5 cl	port or Madeira	4 fl oz
	1 tsp	red wine vinegar	1 tsp
	12.5 cl	unsalted brown or chicken stock (recipes, page 137)	4 fl oz
	4	sheets phyllo pastry, each about 30 cm (12 inches) square	4
	1	egg white, lightly beaten	1
	4	parsley sprigs, for garnish (optional)	4

Peel the pear. (If you like, julienne some of the skin for a garnish and set it aside.) Halve and core the pear, then thinly slice one half, and set the slices aside. Chop the remaining half and set it aside too.

Slice the eye of loin into four equal pieces. Place the pieces between two sheets of plastic film or greaseproof paper; with a meat bat or the flat of a heavy knife, pound the pieces as shown on page 24 to a thickness of about 1 cm (½ inch). Heat the oil in a large, heavy or non-stick frying pan over medium-high heat. Add the lamb medallions and sear them for 1 minute on each side. Remove the medallions from the pan and season them with half the salt and some pepper; set the medallions aside.

Add the ginger, port or Madeira, vinegar and chopped pear to the pan. Lower the heat and simmer the liquid until it is reduced by half — about 7 minutes. Add the stock, the remaining salt and some pepper and return the liquid to a simmer. Transfer the sauce to a food processor or a blender, and purée it. Keep the sauce warm while you prepare the phyllo packages.

Preheat the oven to 220°C (425°F or Mark 7). Fold one of the phyllo sheets in half, keeping the others covered with a damp cloth or plastic film so that they do not become brittle. Pat a lamb medallion dry with a paper towel and position the medallion in the centre of the folded phyllo sheet. Arrange one quarter of the pear slices on top, then fold the phyllo over the meat and fruit. Brush the seams with some of the beaten egg white. Put the phyllo package seam side down on a baking sheet. Brush the top with more egg white. Wrap the remaining lamb medallions and pear slices in the same way.

Bake the packages for 8 minutes for medium-rare lamb. Divide the sauce among four individual plates and set a phyllo package on each plate. Garnish each serving, if you like, with a sprig of parsley and some julienned pear skin.

SUGGESTED ACCOMPANIMENTS: *Brussels sprouts; steamed new potatoes.*

EDITOR'S NOTE: *Only the eye of loin is used here; reserve the fillet for another recipe where lean meat is called for.*

Minced Lamb Pancakes with a Herb Sauce

Serves 6
Working time: about 1 hour and 15 minutes
Total time: about 1 hour and 25 minutes

Calories **345**
Protein **26g**
Cholesterol **85mg**
Total fat **13g**
Saturated fat **4g**
Sodium **270mg**

500 g	lean lamb (from the leg), trimmed of fat and minced (page 43)	1 lb
140 g	plain flour	4½ oz
⅜ tsp	salt	⅜ tsp
1	egg	1
30 cl	light ale	½ pint
1 tbsp	olive oil	1 tbsp
1	onion, finely chopped	1
125 g	mushrooms, chopped	4 oz
6 tbsp	unsalted chicken stock (recipe, page 137)	6 tbsp
	freshly ground black pepper	
2 tbsp	finely sliced spring onion, for garnish	2 tbsp
2 tbsp	finely cut fresh chives, for garnish	2 tbsp
Herb sauce		
45 cl	skimmed milk	¾ pint
1	small onion	1
1	bay leaf	1
1	small blade of mace	1
1	parsley sprig	1
6	black peppercorns	6
30 g	polyunsaturated margarine	1 oz
30 g	plain flour	1 oz
2 tbsp	mixed fresh herbs, or 2 tsp mixed dried herbs	2 tbsp
⅛ tsp	salt	⅛ tsp
	freshly grated nutmeg	
	freshly ground black pepper	

First make the pancake batter. Sift 125 g (4 oz) of the flour with ⅛ teaspoon of the salt into a mixing bowl and make a well in the centre. Break the egg into the centre of the flour, then gradually whisk the egg into the flour. Add the light ale a little at a time, beating well after each addition until the batter is smooth. Cover the bowl and allow the batter to stand while you make the sauce and the filling.

To prepare the sauce, put the milk into a heavy-bottomed saucepan and add the onion, bay leaf, mace, parsley and peppercorns. Heat the milk over medium heat until it almost reaches the boil, then remove it from the heat. Cover the saucepan and let the milk infuse for at least 30 minutes.

Meanwhile, make the lamb filling. Heat half of the olive oil in a large, heavy frying pan over medium heat. Add the onion and cook until it is soft but not brown — 5 to 6 minutes. Increase the heat to high and add the minced lamb. Cook the lamb until it changes colour — 3 to 4 minutes — breaking it up with a wooden spoon as it cooks. Stir in the remaining flour and salt, then add the mushrooms, stock and some black pepper. Bring the mixture to the boil, reduce the heat and simmer, uncovered, for 6 to 8 minutes. Remove the pan from the heat, cover and allow the filling to cool while making the pancakes.

To make the pancakes, heat the remaining olive oil in a 15 cm (6 inch) non-stick frying pan or pancake pan over medium heat. When the oil is hot, pour it out of the pan into a small bowl, leaving just a thin film behind to cover the base of the pan. Stir the pancake batter, then ladle just enough batter into the pan to cover the base, quickly swirling it over the bottom of the pan as you pour it in. Immediately the bottom of the pan is covered with batter, pour the excess batter back into the bowl. Trim off and discard the trail of batter. Cook the pancake until the underside is golden-brown — about 1 minute. Turn it over and brown the other side for 1 minute more. Remove the pancake to a small plate and cover it with a paper towel. Make eleven more pancakes in the same way.

Preheat the oven to 220°C (425°F or Mark 7). Lay the pancakes flat on a work surface and divide the lamb filling between them. Roll each pancake round the filling. Place the filled pancakes in a large ovenproof dish, or two per person in individual gratin dishes.

To complete the sauce, strain the milk through a sieve into a bowl; discard the contents of the sieve. Rinse the saucepan. Melt the margarine in the saucepan over medium heat, stir in the flour and then gradually add the milk. Bring the sauce to the boil, stirring continuously until it thickens. Stir in the mixed herbs and salt, and season with some freshly grated nutmeg and black pepper. Reduce the heat to low and simmer the sauce for 2 to 3 minutes.

Pour the sauce over and round the pancakes. Cook uncovered in the oven until the pancakes are heated through — about 10 minutes. Sprinkle them with the spring onion and chives, and serve immediately.

SUGGESTED ACCOMPANIMENT: *mixed green salad.*

Chili Lamb Tortillas

Serves 4
Working time: about 50 minutes
Total time: about 3 hours and 30 minutes (includes soaking)

Calories **385**
Protein **28g**
Cholesterol **40mg**
Total fat **12g**
Saturated fat **4g**
Sodium **240mg**

250 g	lean lamb (from the loin), trimmed of fat and finely diced	8 oz
175 g	dried borlotti beans or pinto beans, picked over	6 oz
1 tbsp	safflower oil	1 tbsp
2	onions, chopped	2
1	sweet red pepper, seeded, deribbed and chopped	1
1	garlic clove, chopped	1
3	tomatoes, skinned, seeded and chopped	3
1	green chili pepper, seeded and chopped (caution, page 83)	1
2 tbsp	tomato paste	2 tbsp
15 cl	unsalted brown stock (recipe, page 137)	¼ pint
¼ tsp	salt	¼ tsp
	freshly ground black pepper	
Tortilla dough		
90 g	plain flour	3 oz
⅛ tsp	salt	⅛ tsp
15 g	hard white vegetable fat	½ oz

Rinse the beans under cold running water, then put them into a large, heavy saucepan and pour in enough cold water to cover them by about 7.5 cm (3 inches). Discard any beans that float to the surface. Cover the pan, leaving the lid ajar, and slowly bring the liquid to the boil. Boil the beans for 2 minutes, then turn off the heat and soak the beans, covered, for at least 1 hour. (Alternatively, soak the beans overnight in cold water.)

Discard the soaking liquid and rinse the beans. Pour in enough cold water to cover them by about 7.5 cm

(3 inches). Boil the beans for 10 minutes, then reduce the heat and simmer them until they are tender — 1 to 2 hours. Drain and rinse under cold running water.

To make the tortillas, sift the flour and salt into a bowl and rub in the fat until the mixture resembles fine breadcrumbs. Add 3 to 4 tablespoons of warm water, enough to form a stiff dough, and mix well. Turn the dough on to a floured surface and knead until it is smooth — about 2 minutes. Divide the dough into four equal pieces, form each quarter into a ball with your hands, and roll it out on a lightly floured surface to an 18 cm (7 inch) circle.

Heat a heavy frying pan and fry a tortilla over high heat until its surface bubbles and the underside begins to brown — about 30 seconds. Turn it over and cook the other side until it is pale brown — about another 30 seconds. Immediately place it over an inverted dariole mould, so that it will cool and harden in a cupped shape. Cook and shape the remaining tortillas; remove them from the moulds when cool.

To make the chili, heat the oil in a sauté pan over medium heat. Add the lamb and seal it by stirring it until it changes colour. Reduce the heat, add the onions, red pepper and garlic and sauté them gently until the onions soften — about 5 minutes. Add the tomatoes, chili pepper, tomato paste and stock; season with the salt and some black pepper. Cover the pan and cook for 10 minutes. Then stir in the beans and heat them through. Keep the chili warm. Meanwhile, preheat the oven to 180°C (350°F or Mark 4).

Fit the tortillas over the moulds again and heat in the oven for 10 minutes. Then place them on a serving dish, fill with the lamb chili and serve immediately.

SUGGESTED ACCOMPANIMENT: *tomato and avocado salad.*
EDITOR'S NOTE: *The lamb may be minced instead of diced.*

Sweet Pepper and Lamb Lasagne

Serves 6
Working time: about 45 minutes
Total time: about 1 hour and 45 minutes

Calories **315**
Protein **25g**
Cholesterol **50mg**
Total fat **10g**
Saturated fat **4g**
Sodium **290mg**

350 g	lean lamb (from the leg), trimmed of fat and minced (page 43)	12 oz
1	onion, chopped	1
1	garlic clove, chopped	1
2	sticks celery, chopped	2
2 tbsp	tomato paste	2 tbsp
12.5 cl	red wine	4 fl oz
12.5 cl	unsalted brown or chicken stock (recipes, page 137)	4 fl oz
1	bay leaf	1
½ tsp	salt	½ tsp
	freshly ground black pepper	
9	lasagne strips	9
30 g	polyunsaturated margarine	1 oz
30 g	plain flour	1 oz
30 cl	skimmed milk	½ pint
30 g	Parmesan cheese, grated	1 oz
	white pepper	

Sweet pepper sauce		
3	sweet peppers (one each green, red and yellow), seeded and sliced	3
30 cl	passata	½ pint
2	garlic cloves, crushed	2
1 tsp	chopped fresh thyme, or ¼ tsp dried thyme	1 tsp
1 tsp	chopped fresh oregano, or ¼ tsp dried oregano	1 tsp
½ tbsp	cornflour	½ tbsp

Heat a heavy, non-stick sauté pan over medium heat and cook the lamb, stirring, until the meat is sealed and separated — 3 to 4 minutes. Add the onion and continue stirring until it is soft — about 3 minutes. Add the garlic, celery, tomato paste, wine, stock and bay leaf; season with the salt and some pepper. Cover, and cook over low heat for 30 minutes.

Meanwhile, make the sweet pepper sauce. Put the sliced sweet peppers, passata, garlic, thyme and oregano into a heavy-bottomed saucepan, cover and simmer for 15 minutes. Then blend the cornflour with 2 tablespoons of water, add it to the sweet pepper mixture and stir until the sauce thickens — 1 to 2 minutes. Set the sauce aside.

While the sauce is simmering bring 3 litres (5 pints) of water to the boil. Add the lasagne strips and boil for 7 minutes — the pasta will be slightly undercooked. Drain the pasta and spread it on a clean tea towel to dry. Preheat the oven to 190°C (375°F or Mark 5).

When the meat mixture is cooked, arrange three strips of lasagne in the bottom of a 30 by 20 cm (12 by 8 inch) baking dish. Spread the sweet pepper sauce evenly over the lasagne, then make a second layer of pasta with three more strips of lasagne. Cover this with the lamb mixture and arrange the remaining strips of lasagne on top.

To make a gratin topping, melt the margarine in a saucepan over medium heat. Add the flour and stir for 1 minute, then gradually add the milk, stirring continuously, and cook for 3 minutes. Stir in half of the grated Parmesan and season with white pepper.

Pour the topping evenly over the lasagne. Sprinkle it with the remaining Parmesan and bake until golden-brown — 40 to 45 minutes.

SUGGESTED ACCOMPANIMENT: *green salad.*

EDITOR'S NOTE: Passata — literally "mashed" in Italian — is the sieved flesh of ripe red tomatoes; it is available in many supermarkets. If it is not obtainable, substitute 800 g (1¾ lb) canned tomatoes; discard the juice and sieve the flesh.

Mongolian Stuffed Dumplings

Serves 4
Working time: about 1 hour and 15 minutes
Total time: about 2 hours

Calories **390**
Protein **24g**
Cholesterol **100mg**
Total fat **8g**
Saturated fat **3g**
Sodium **220mg**

250 g	lean lamb (from the leg or loin), trimmed of fat and minced (page 43)	8 oz
1 tsp	freshly ground allspice, plus a little for garnish	1 tsp
½ tsp	salt	½ tsp
	freshly ground black pepper	
300 g	ripe purple plums, stoned	10 oz
1 tbsp	light brown sugar	1 tbsp
1 ½ tsp	fruit vinegar	1 ½ tsp
175 g	thick Greek yogurt	6 oz
Dumpling dough		
250 g	strong plain flour	8 oz
⅛ tsp	salt	⅛ tsp
1	egg, beaten	1

First make the dumpling dough. Sift the flour and salt into a mixing bowl and form a well in the centre. Pour the beaten egg and 5 tablespoons of cold water into the well and gradually incorporate the flour into the liquid to form a stiff dough. You may need an additional tablespoon of water; add just enough to make a ball of dough that is pliable but not crumbly. Knead the dough on a floured surface until it stretches when pulled apart — about 10 minutes. Cover and leave it to rest in a cool place for 30 minutes.

In a mixing bowl, beat the teaspoon of allspice, the salt and some pepper into the minced lamb. Knead it well and set it aside.

Reserve two of the plums. Simmer the rest, covered, with the sugar and 1 tablespoon of water in a heavy-bottomed, non-reactive saucepan until the fruit is tender and the skins soft — 15 to 20 minutes. Purée the cooked plums in a blender or food processor with the stewing juice and the fruit vinegar. Beat two thirds of the plum purée into the minced lamb and set the remainder aside for the sauce.

Divide the dumpling dough in two equal halves. Form each piece of dough into a ball. Roll out one ball to a thickness of about 2 mm (1/16 inch) on a lightly floured surface. Using a 7.5 cm (3 inch) circular plain biscuit cutter, cut out 12 circles. Repeat the procedure with the second ball of dough. Spoon a little of the lamb and plum filling in the centre of a dough circle. Dampen the edges of the dough, pull them up and press them firmly together, forming a semi-circular dumpling with a scalloped top. Fill and seal all the dough circles in the same way.

Pour enough water into a saucepan to fill it 2.5 cm (1 inch) deep. Set a steamer over the pan and bring the water to the boil. Brush the base of the steamer lightly with oil and add the dumplings, leaving a little space around each one. Cover the steamer and steam the dumplings for 15 minutes.

While the dumplings are steaming, prepare the dressings. Finely dice the reserved plums, then gently heat them through with the reserved plum purée in a non-reactive saucepan. Heat the yogurt in a bowl set over a saucepan of gently simmering water. Season it with black pepper.

Serve the stuffed dumplings piping hot in heated individual bowls, dressed with some of the warm yogurt and the hot plum sauce, plus a light sprinkling of freshly ground allspice.

SUGGESTED ACCOMPANIMENT: *chicory and watercress salad.*

Burghul Layered with Lamb and Fruit

Serves 6
Working time: about 30 minutes
Total time: about 1 hour and 45 minutes

Calories **350**
Protein **30g**
Cholesterol **75mg**
Total fat **13g**
Saturated fat **4g**
Sodium **335mg**

600 g	thin lamb slices (from the fillet end of the leg), trimmed of fat and flattened into escalopes 3 mm (⅛ inch) thick (page 24)	1 ¼ lb
1 tsp	virgin olive oil	1 tsp
1	small onion, sliced	1
1 tsp	salt	1 tsp
	freshly ground black pepper	
90 g	dried apricots, thoroughly rinsed	3 oz
1 tsp	ground cinnamon	1 tsp
½ tsp	ground coriander	½ tsp
250 g	burghul	8 oz
2 tbsp	finely chopped mint	2 tbsp
60 g	raisins	2 oz
90 g	fresh dates, stoned and halved	3 oz

Heat the oil in a large, heavy frying pan until it is very hot but not smoking. Quickly brown the lamb slices — about 30 seconds on each side — and transfer them to a fireproof casserole or saucepan. Reduce the heat, put the onion in the frying pan and cook it, stirring, for 2 to 3 minutes, until it softens. Season the lamb slices with ½ teaspoon of the salt and a little pepper, then add the onion to the casserole, together with the apricots, cinnamon and coriander. Cover the contents of the casserole with boiling water and simmer for 1 hour or until tender.

While the meat is cooking, soak the burghul in twice its volume of cold water for 30 minutes. Strain off any residual liquid, add the mint and the remaining ½ teaspoon of salt to the burghul and stir well.

Add the raisins and halved dates to the casserole and allow them to warm through — 2 to 3 minutes. Strain the stock from the casserole through a sieve into a saucepan. Boil it rapidly until only about 12.5 cl (4 fl oz) of liquid remains, then pour the reduced stock back on to the meat and fruit.

Layer the soaked burghul and the lamb mixture in a 1.5 litre (2½ pint) heatproof casserole, beginning and ending with a layer of burghul. Place a four-fold layer of muslin over the top of the burghul and seal the top of the casserole with aluminium foil. Put the casserole on a trivet inside a larger pot and pour boiling water into the outer pot to a depth of about 5 cm (2 inches). Cover the outer pot and steam gently for about 30 minutes. Remove the muslin and foil, and serve the dish hot from the casserole.

SUGGESTED ACCOMPANIMENT: *lightly steamed leaf spinach.*

Lamb and Orange Pilaff

Serves 4
Working time: about 30 minutes
Total time: about 1 hour and 25 minutes

Calories **385**
Protein **16g**
Cholesterol **55mg**
Total fat **8g**
Saturated fat **3g**
Sodium **205mg**

350 g	lean lamb (from the leg or loin), trimmed of fat and finely diced	12 oz
1 tsp	safflower oil	1 tsp
1	onion, chopped	1
1	large leek, trimmed, washed and sliced	1
200 g	long-grain brown rice	7 oz
45 cl	unsalted brown or chicken stock (recipes, page 137)	¾ pint
1 tsp	chopped fresh rosemary, or ½ tsp dried rosemary	1 tsp
¼ tsp	salt	¼ tsp
	freshly ground black pepper	
1	orange, rind grated and flesh cut into segments	1
2	carrots, peeled	2
125 g	courgettes, trimmed	4 oz
30 g	raisins	1 oz

Preheat the oven to 180°C (350°F or Mark 4).

Heat the oil in a fireproof casserole over high heat. Add the lamb and sear it quickly on all sides. Stir in the onion, leek and rice and cook them for 1 minute. Add the stock, rosemary, salt, pepper and orange rind. Bring the mixture to the boil, then cover the casserole, transfer it to the oven and bake the pilaff until the rice is almost tender and the liquid virtually absorbed — about 40 minutes.

Using a potato peeler, shred the carrots and courgettes into long strips. Reserve a few carrot strips for garnish and stir the remainder into the lamb mixture along with the courgette strips and the raisins. Return the casserole to the oven and cook, covered, until the rice and carrots are tender — about 20 minutes. Stir in the orange segments and garnish with the reserved carrot ribbons just before serving.

Kibbeh with Coriander Sauce

THE MANY VARIATIONS ON THIS LEBANESE DISH ARE ALL MADE
WITH A SPICED CRUST OF BURGHUL AND MINCED LAMB.

Serves 4
Working time: about 40 minutes
Total time: about 1 hour and 25 minutes

Calories **335**
Protein **38g**
Cholesterol **75mg**
Total fat **14g**
Saturated fat **5g**
Sodium **390mg**

175 g	lean lamb (from the leg or loin), trimmed of fat and minced (page 43)	6 oz
125 g	burghul	4 oz
1	onion, quartered	1
15 g	parsley	½ oz
2	garlic cloves, one coarsely chopped, one crushed	2
½ tsp	ground cinnamon	½ tsp
½ tsp	ground allspice	½ tsp
½ tsp	salt	½ tsp
	freshly ground black pepper	
12.5 cl	plain low-fat yogurt	4 fl oz
1 tsp	fresh lemon juice	1 tsp
½ tsp	ground coriander	½ tsp
	fresh coriander sprigs, for garnish	
Lamb and pine-nut filling		
175 g	lean lamb (from the leg or loin), trimmed of fat and minced (page 43)	6 oz
1 tsp	virgin olive oil	1 tsp
1	onion, chopped	1
1	garlic clove, chopped	1
2 tbsp	pine-nuts	2 tbsp
1 tsp	ground cinnamon	1 tsp
½ tsp	ground allspice	½ tsp
2 tsp	fresh lemon juice	2 tsp
¼ tsp	salt	¼ tsp
	freshly ground black pepper	

Put the burghul in a heatproof bowl and pour 60 cl (1 pint) of boiling water over it. Let the burghul soak for 20 minutes, then drain it in a sieve, pressing out as much liquid as possible with the back of a spoon. Put the onion, parsley and the coarsely chopped garlic in a food processor and process just long enough to chop them up. Add the burghul and the lamb, along with the cinnamon and allspice, all but a pinch of the salt and plenty of pepper. Blend until all the ingredients are mixed and well bound together. Set the mixture aside.

To make the filling, heat the oil in a frying pan and soften the chopped onion over medium heat. Add the garlic and lamb and fry, stirring constantly, until the meat begins to brown — 4 to 5 minutes. Add the pine-nuts and continue to fry for 2 minutes. Stir in the cinnamon, allspice, lemon juice, salt and some pepper, and cook for 1 minute more. Set the filling aside.

Preheat the oven to 190°C (375°F or Mark 5), and grease a 20 cm (8 inch) flan dish or spring-form tin. Spread half of the lamb and burghul mixture smoothly over the bottom of the dish. Cover the mixture with the lamb and pine-nut filling, pressing it down well, then spread the remaining burghul mixture over the top. Smooth the surface with a palette knife and lightly inscribe cutting lines for eight wedge-shaped sections. Brush the surface with a little olive oil, and bake the *kibbeh* until it is brown — 35 to 45 minutes.

For the coriander sauce, mix together the yogurt, 1 teaspoon of lemon juice, the crushed garlic clove, ground coriander, some black pepper and the remaining pinch of salt. Serve the *kibbeh* hot or cold with the sauce, garnished with fresh coriander sprigs.

SUGGESTED ACCOMPANIMENT: *white cabbage and radish salad in a lemon and cardamom dressing.*

20 cl	unsalted brown or chicken stock, (recipes, page 137)	7 fl oz
	Dill sauce	
6 tbsp	thick Greek yogurt	6 tbsp
4 tbsp	plain low-fat yogurt	4 tbsp
2 tbsp	finely cut fresh dill	2 tbsp
⅛ tsp	salt	⅛ tsp
	freshly ground black pepper	

Place the lentils in a saucepan and cover them with water, bring the water to the boil then reduce the heat and simmer them until they are tender — about 20 minutes. Drain the lentils thoroughly, then transfer them to a bowl and allow them to cool.

Add the minced lamb to the lentils, together with the dill, grated onion, garlic, turmeric, nutmeg, egg white, salt and some black pepper. Knead well with your hands until all the ingredients are evenly combined and stick together — about 5 minutes.

Put the dried apricots, sunflower seeds, sultanas and lemon juice in a separate bowl and mix them well together. Divide the meat mixture in half on a dampened board and flatten each half into an oval about 2 cm (¾ inch) thick. Shape the stuffing into two smaller ovals and place one in the centre of each oval of meat. With your hands, shape the meat mixture around the stuffing to cover it completely.

Heat the oil in a deep, non-stick sauté pan. Fry the lamb loaves over moderate heat until they are lightly browned all over — about 5 minutes. Remove them carefully from the pan and set them aside. Wipe the pan clean with a paper towel, then add the chopped onion. Return the pan to the heat and dry-fry until the onion is browned — about 5 minutes.

Stir in the stock and bring it to the boil, then lower the heat and add the meat loaves. Cover and simmer gently for 45 minutes to 1 hour, carefully turning them once during this time so that they cook evenly.

To make the dill sauce, mix together the Greek and plain yogurt, stir in the dill and season with the salt and some freshly ground pepper.

Remove the loaves from the pan, slice them with a sharp knife, then arrange them on a warm serving platter. Serve immediately with the sauce.

SUGGESTED ACCOMPANIMENT: *a salad of watercress, chicory and orange.*

Lamb Loaf Stuffed with Dried Apricots

Serves 6
Working time: about 1 hour
Total time: about 2 hours

Calories **290**	500 g	lean lamb (from the leg), trimmed of fat and minced (page 43)	1 lb
Protein **27g**			
Cholesterol **80mg**	100 g	split red lentils	3½ oz
Total fat **10g**	4 tbsp	finely cut fresh dill	4 tbsp
Saturated fat **3g**	2 tbsp	grated onion	2 tbsp
Sodium **270mg**	3	garlic cloves, crushed	3
	2 tsp	ground turmeric	2 tsp
	¼ tsp	freshly grated nutmeg	¼ tsp
	1	large egg white, lightly beaten	1
	½ tsp	salt	½ tsp
		freshly ground black pepper	
	100 g	dried apricots, finely chopped	3½ oz
	2 tbsp	sunflower seeds	2 tbsp
	1 tbsp	finely chopped sultanas	1 tbsp
	1 tbsp	fresh lemon juice	1 tbsp
	1 tbsp	safflower oil	1 tbsp
	1	large onion, finely chopped	1

Loin Chop and Artichoke Gratin

Serves 8
Working time: about 25 minutes
Total time: about 50 minutes

Calories **225**
Protein **23g**
Cholesterol **75mg**
Total fat **14g**
Saturated fat **6g**
Sodium **205mg**

8	loin chops (about 100 g/5 oz each), trimmed of fat	8
12	garlic cloves, peeled	12
1 tbsp	virgin olive oil	1 tbsp
1 tsp	fresh thyme, or ½ tsp dried thyme	1 tsp
½ tsp	salt	½ tsp
	freshly ground black pepper	
3	large globe artichokes	3
½ tsp	lemon	½ tsp
30 g	Parmesan cheese, grated	1 oz
15 g	fresh white breadcrumbs	½ oz
1 tbsp	chopped fresh parsley	1 tbsp

Preheat the oven to 200°C (400°F or Mark 6).

Arrange the chops in the base of a shallow oven-proof dish, interspersing them with the garlic cloves. Brush the chops with the oil, sprinkle them with the thyme and season with the salt and some black pepper. Cook, uncovered, in the oven for 15 minutes.

Meanwhile, prepare the artichokes. Bring a saucepan of water to the boil. Break off the stalks from the artichokes and remove the bottom three to four rows of tough outer leaves. Trim off the dark green base of each artichoke using a paring knife. Cut the top 4 cm (1½ inches) off each artichoke and discard, then pull out the densely packed central leaves to expose the hairy choke. Scoop out the chokes with a teaspoon. While working on the artichokes, rub them frequently with the cut surface of the half lemon to prevent them from discolouring.

Squeeze the juice remaining in the lemon half into the boiling water. Add the artichokes and cook them until tender — about 5 minutes. Drain them well and cut them into eighths or slices.

Remove the chops from the oven, and increase the temperature to 220°C (425°F or Mark 7). Skim off any fat from the juices in the cooking dish. Distribute the artichokes evenly over and around the chops. Combine the Parmesan and the breadcrumbs, then sprinkle this mixture over the chops and artichokes. Return the dish to the oven until the chops are well cooked and the topping is golden-brown — 20 to 25 minutes. Sprinkle with the parsley and serve.

SUGGESTED ACCOMPANIMENTS: *tomato and French bean salad; hot French bread.*

Moussaka

Serves 6

Working time: about 1 hour and 10 minutes

Total time: about 2 hours and 30 minutes

Calories **380**
Protein **30g**
Cholesterol **90mg**
Total fat **14g**
Saturated fat **6g**
Sodium **370mg**

500 g	lean lamb (from the leg), trimmed of fat and minced (page 43)	1 lb
2	onions, chopped	2
2	garlic cloves, crushed	2
500 g	ripe tomatoes, roughly chopped	1 lb
20 cl	red wine	7 fl oz
2 tbsp	tomato paste	2 tbsp
1	green chili pepper, halved, seeded and finely chopped (caution, page 83)	1
2 tbsp	chopped parsley	2 tbsp
1 tbsp	chopped fresh marjoram, or 1½ tsp dried marjoram	1 tbsp
1	bay leaf	1
¼ tsp	freshly grated nutmeg	¼ tsp
¾ tsp	salt	¾ tsp
	freshly ground black pepper	
750 g	aubergines, trimmed and thinly sliced	1½ lb
250 g	potatoes, thinly sliced	8 oz
30 g	Parmesan cheese, freshly grated	1 oz
White sauce		
60 g	polyunsaturated margarine	2 oz
60 g	plain flour	2 oz
30 cl	skimmed milk	½ pint
½ tsp	freshly grated nutmeg	½ tsp
⅛ tsp	salt	⅛ tsp
30 cl	plain low-fat yogurt	½ pint

Lightly brush a non-stick frying pan with oil and heat it over medium heat. Add the minced lamb and cook it, stirring constantly, until it changes colour — 3 to 4 minutes. Add the onions and continue stirring for a fur-ther 5 minutes. Add the garlic, tomatoes, wine, tomato paste, chili pepper, parsley, marjoram, bay leaf and nutmeg. Season with ¼ teaspoon of the salt and some freshly ground pepper. Continue stirring until the mix-ture comes to the boil, then reduce the heat, cover, and simmer gently for 40 minutes.

Meanwhile, sprinkle the aubergine slices with the remaining ½ teaspoon of salt. Leave them to stand for 20 minutes, then rinse them under cold running water to remove the salt.

Pour enough water into a saucepan to fill it 2.5 cm (1 inch) deep. Set a vegetable steamer in the pan and bring the water to the boil. Put the aubergine slices in the steamer, cover the saucepan tightly and steam the aubergines until tender — about 10 minutes. While they are steaming, boil the potato slices in unsalted water until tender — about 5 minutes. Drain well.

Preheat the oven to 180°C (350°F or Mark 4). Cover the bottom of a 28 by 22 cm (11 by 9 inch) baking dish with the potato slices. Cover the potatoes with half of the aubergines, then add the meat mixture. Arrange the remaining aubergine slices in a layer on top.

To make the sauce, melt the margarine in a heavy-bottomed saucepan over medium heat, add the flour and stir for 1 minute. Gradually add the milk, stirring continuously, then add the nutmeg and the salt. Con-tinue stirring the sauce until it thickens — 3 to 4 minutes. Remove from the heat and stir in the yogurt.

Pour the sauce over the moussaka, then sprinkle on the Parmesan cheese. Bake the moussaka in the oven until golden-brown and bubbling — 40 to 50 minutes. Serve hot, straight from the dish.

SUGGESTED ACCOMPANIMENT: *mixed green salad.*

Lamb and Chicory Gratin

Serves 4
Working time: about 45 minutes
Total time: about 1 hour and 30 minutes

Calories **335**
Protein **35g**
Cholesterol **95mg**
Total fat **16g**
Saturated fat **7g**
Sodium **335mg**

1 kg	loin, boned and trimmed of fat, eye only (page 134)	2¼ lb
1 tbsp	fresh lemon juice	1 tbsp
4	heads of chicory, trimmed	4
2 tsp	safflower oil	2 tsp
4	shallots, or 1 small onion, thinly sliced	4
1 tbsp	plain flour	1 tbsp
17.5 cl	unsalted brown or chicken stock (recipes, page 137)	6 fl oz
1 tbsp	Dijon mustard	1 tbsp
	freshly ground black pepper	
50 g	dry breadcrumbs	1½ oz
125 g	low-fat mozzarella cheese, grated	4 oz

Bring 1 litre (1¾ pints) of water to the boil in a large saucepan. Add the lemon juice and chicory and cook them for 5 minutes. Drain the chicory and rinse it under cold running water. When the chicory is cool enough to handle, squeeze out the liquid with your hands. Quarter each chicory lengthwise and set the pieces aside.

Preheat the oven to 200°C (400°F or Mark 6).

Slice the eye of loin into eight pieces. Place the slices between two pieces of plastic film or greaseproof paper and pound them with a meat bat or the flat of a heavy knife until they are only about 5 mm (¼ inch) thick (page 24). Heat the oil in a large, heavy or non-stick sauté pan over high heat. Add the lamb slices and cook them for 30 seconds on each side. Remove the slices from the pan and set them aside.

Reduce the heat to medium. Add the shallot or onion slices to the pan; cook them, stirring con-tinuously, until they have browned — about 5 minutes. Remove the pan from the heat and stir in the flour. Whisking constantly, pour in the stock in a slow, steady stream. Return the pan to the heat and cook the sauce, stirring, until it thickens — about 2 minutes. Mix in the mustard and a generous grinding of pepper, then simmer the sauce for 5 minutes more.

Sprinkle 1 tablespoon of the breadcrumbs into a 20 cm (8 inch) baking or gratin dish. Place the lamb slices on top of the crumbs and spread the chicory quarters over the lamb. Pour the sauce over all; sprinkle the mozzarella and remaining breadcrumbs on top. Bake the gratin until the liquid bubbles and the top has browned — about 40 minutes.

SUGGESTED ACCOMPANIMENTS: *steamed asparagus; toasted French bread.*

EDITOR'S NOTE: *Only the eye of the loin is used here; reserve the fillet for another recipe where lean meat is called for.*

Layered Lamb Bake with Fennel

Serves 6
Working time: about 45 minutes
Total time: about 1 hour and 30 minutes

Calories **350**
Protein **29g**
Cholesterol **75mg**
Total fat **14g**
Saturated fat **6g**
Sodium **390mg**

6	loin chops (about 150 g/5 oz each), trimmed of fat	6
850 g	potatoes, peeled and thinly sliced	1¾ lb
8 cl	skimmed milk	3 fl oz
400 g	courgettes, trimmed and thinly sliced	14 oz
850 g	bulb fennel, trimmed and thinly sliced, trimmings reserved	1¾ lb
½ tsp	salt	½ tsp
¾ tsp	ground nutmeg	¾ tsp
	freshly ground black pepper	
20 g	polyunsaturated margarine, melted	¾ oz
3 tsp	grated lemon rind	3 tsp
2 tsp	chopped bulb fennel tops	2 tsp
	lemon wedges, for garnish	
	sprigs of bulb fennel tops, for garnish	

Preheat the oven to 220°C (425°F or Mark 7).

Rinse the potato slices in cold water and pat them dry with paper towels. Pour half of the milk into a shallow 1.75 litre (3 pint) ovenproof dish. Arrange one third of the potato slices over the base of the dish. Cover the potato slices with half of the courgettes, and top these with half of the fennel. Season with one third of the salt, half of the nutmeg and some pepper. Over the fennel, layer half of the remaining potatoes and then the remaining courgettes and fennel. Season as before and add the remaining milk. Top the dish with overlapping slices of potato, brush them evenly with the margarine and cover with foil. Bake the vegetables in the oven for 30 minutes.

Meanwhile, prepare the chops. Mix together the remaining third of the salt, some pepper and the lemon rind. Rub a little of this mixture over both sides of the chops. Secure the chops into neat rounds with cocktail sticks. Chop the reserved fennel trimmings and stuff a teaspoon of the chopped fennel into the space between the flap and fillet of each chop.

Arrange the chops on top of the vegetables and return to the oven, uncovered, for 20 to 30 minutes for rare to medium meat. Remove the cocktail sticks. Serve garnished with lemon wedges and fennel sprigs.

EDITOR'S NOTE: *Kohlrabi or sweet white potatoes can be substituted for the potatoes.*

Lamb and Aubergine Terrine

Serves 8
Working time: about 1 hour and 20 minutes
Total time: about 9 hours (includes chilling)

Calories **255**
Protein **31g**
Cholesterol **75mg**
Total fat **12g**
Saturated fat **5g**
Sodium **170mg**

1.25 kg	leg of lamb (fillet end), boned, trimmed of fat, cut into 5 mm (¼ inch) thick slices	2½ lb
2	sweet red peppers	2
2 tbsp	virgin olive oil	2 tbsp
1	onion, chopped	1
3	garlic cloves, thinly sliced	3
½ tbsp	chopped fresh oregano, or ½ tsp dried oregano	½ tbsp
½ tbsp	fresh thyme, or ½ tsp dried thyme	½ tbsp
½ tsp	salt	½ tsp
	freshly ground black pepper	
850 g	canned unsalted whole tomatoes, drained, or 600 g (1¼ lb) ripe tomatoes, skinned, seeded and chopped	1¾ lb
2 tbsp	red wine vinegar	2 tbsp
1	large aubergine (about 600 g/1¼ lb)	1
½ tsp	fresh lemon juice	½ tsp

Grill the peppers, turning them with tongs as they blister, until their skins are blackened all over — about 15 minutes. Transfer the peppers to a bowl and cover it with plastic film. When the peppers are cool enough to handle, skin, seed and coarsely chop them, reserving their juice.

Heat ½ tablespoon of the oil in a heavy-bottomed saucepan over medium-low heat. Add the onion, garlic, oregano, thyme, ¼ teaspoon of the salt and some black pepper. Cook the mixture, stirring occasionally, until the onion is translucent — about 5 minutes. Add the tomatoes, the peppers and their juice, and the

vinegar. Simmer the sauce until it has thickened — about 7 minutes. Purée the sauce in a food processor or a blender and return it to the pan.

Preheat the grill. With a small, sharp knife, remove four long strips of skin from the aubergine; each strip should be about 1 cm (½ inch) wide. Set the strips aside. Slice the aubergine lengthwise into 5 mm (¼ inch) slices. Place the slices on a large, non-reactive baking sheet, sprinkle them with the lemon juice and the remaining ¼ teaspoon of salt and grill them for 5 minutes. Set the slices aside until you are ready to assemble the terrine.

Place the slices of lamb between plastic film or greaseproof paper and pound them with a meat bat or the flat of a heavy knife to a thickness of about 3 mm (⅛ inch) as shown on page 24.

Heat 1 tablespoon of the remaining oil in a large, non-stick frying pan over high heat. Add one quarter of the lamb slices and sauté them for 30 seconds each side. Remove the slices and sauté a second batch; set the second batch aside. Pour the remaining ½ tablespoon of oil into the pan and sauté the remaining lamb slices in two final batches. After removing the last slices from the pan, pour in 4 tablespoons of water and stir to dislodge any caramelized juices; add this liquid to the tomato sauce.

Preheat the oven to 170°C (325°F or Mark 3). Lightly oil a 2 litre (3½ pint) non-reactive loaf tin. Arrange the strips of aubergine skin in a crisscross pattern in the bottom, their shiny sides down. Place a layer of aubergine slices on top, followed by a layer of the lamb slices and about 4 tablespoons of the sauce. Repeat the layering process until all the slices have been used, topping the terrine with a layer of aubergine. Reserve any remaining sauce.

Cover the top of the terrine with greaseproof paper and set the terrine in the oven. To prevent the lamb slices from curling during cooking, weight the top of the terrine by placing another loaf tin filled part way with dried beans on top of the terrine.

Bake the terrine for 45 minutes. Remove the weight from the top and continue baking the terrine until the meat is tender — about 45 minutes more. Remove the terrine from the oven and allow it to stand at room temperature for 30 minutes. Then put it in the refrigerator and chill it for at least 6 hours.

To unmould the terrine, run a knife around the inside of the tin, then remove the greaseproof paper and invert a platter over the top. Turn tin and platter over together. Wrap the terrine for a few seconds in a hot, wet tea towel, then carefully lift away the tin. Serve the terrine in slices, with any reserved sauce.

SUGGESTED ACCOMPANIMENTS: *lettuce and cucumber salad; pitta bread.*

Aubergine Fans

Serves 4
Working time: about 25 minutes
Total time: about 1 hour

Calories **200**
Protein **23g**
Cholesterol **60mg**
Total fat **10g**
Saturated fat **6g**
Sodium **400mg**

250 g	lean lamb (from the leg or loin), trimmed of fat and minced (page 43)	8 oz
2	aubergines (about 250g/8 oz each), stalks removed	2
60 g	bulb fennel, trimmed and finely chopped	2 oz
½ tsp	dried fennel seeds, lightly crushed	½ tsp
1 tbsp	tomato paste	1 tbsp
4	tomatoes, skinned, two chopped, two sliced	4
¼ tsp	salt	¼ tsp
	freshly ground black pepper	
125 g	low-fat mozzarella cheese, thinly sliced	4 oz

Halve the aubergines lengthwise. Lay one half aubergine, cut side down, on a board. Using a sharp knife, cut several horizontal slices 5 mm (¼ inch) apart, leaving a hinge of flesh about 1 cm (½ inch) wide at the stalk end. Trim off and discard the top slice. Cut the remaining half aubergines into fans in the same way. Place the fans in a shallow baking dish.

Preheat the oven to 190°C (375°F or Mark 5). Heat a non-stick frying pan over medium heat, put in the lamb and cook it for 3 minutes, stirring to sear it all over. Stir in the chopped fennel and cook for a further 1 minute, then add the fennel seeds, tomato paste, chopped tomatoes, salt and some pepper. Stir well and remove the pan from the heat.

Using a teaspoon, spoon the lamb mixture between the slices of the aubergine fans, then cover each layer of meat filling with mozzarella or tomato slices, alternating the toppings. Cover the dish with foil and bake for 20 minutes, then bake uncovered until the aubergines are tender and the cheese is golden-brown — about 20 minutes.

SUGGESTED ACCOMPANIMENT: *steamed mange-tout and baby sweetcorn.*

Potatoes with a Spiced Lamb Stuffing

Serves 4
Working time: about 40 minutes
Total time: about 1 hour and 40 minutes

Calories **270**
Protein **14g**
Cholesterol **25mg**
Total fat **5g**
Saturated fat **2g**
Sodium **230mg**

150 g	lean lamb (from the leg), trimmed of fat and minced (page 43)	5 oz
8	even-sized potatoes (about 100 g/ 3½ oz each), scrubbed	8
1	small onion, finely chopped	1
1	garlic clove, crushed	1
1 tbsp	raisins, rinsed and finely chopped	1 tbsp
1 tbsp	pine-nuts, roughly chopped	1 tbsp
1 tsp	ground cinnamon	1 tsp
½ tsp	ground allspice	½ tsp
½ tsp	ground turmeric	½ tsp
2 tbsp	tomato paste	2 tbsp
¼ tsp	salt	¼ tsp
	freshly ground black pepper	
6 tbsp	unsalted brown or chicken stock (recipes, page 137)	6 tbsp
1 tbsp	crème fraîche	1 tbsp

Preheat the oven to 200°C (400°F or Mark 6).

Make a 1 cm (½ inch) deep horizontal slit about one quarter of the way down each potato. Bake them in the oven until they are tender — about 1 hour.

Meanwhile, make the stuffing. Lightly brush a non-stick frying pan with oil and heat it over medium heat. Stir-fry the onion until it is brown — about 5 minutes. Add the minced lamb and continue stir-frying until it changes colour — 3 to 4 minutes — then add the garlic, raisins, pine-nuts, cinnamon, allspice, turmeric, tomato paste, salt and some freshly ground pepper. Stir for 1 minute, then add the stock and continue cooking the mixture for a further 5 minutes, stirring regularly. Set the stuffing aside.

When the potatoes are cool enough to handle, slice off their tops and hollow out their insides with a teaspoon, taking care not to puncture their skins; leave a shell of about 5 mm (¼ inch) on each potato. Mash half of the scooped-out potato with the *crème fraîche*. (Reserve the remaining potato and the tops for another use.) Spoon the mashed potato into the potato shells, pressing down in the centre to make a well for the lamb stuffing. Fill the shells with the stuffing and return them to the oven to heat through — about 10 minutes. Serve immediately.

SUGGESTED ACCOMPANIMENT: *green salad.*

Baked Stuffed Onions

Serves 4
Working time: about 30 minutes
Total time: about 1 hour and 10 minutes

Calories **215**
Protein **25g**
Cholesterol **75mg**
Total Fat **10g**
Saturated fat **3g**
Sodium **170mg**

350 g	lean lamb (from the leg or loin), trimmed of fat and minced (page 43)	12 oz
4	large Spanish onions (about 250 g/ 8 oz each)	4
125 g	celeriac, peeled and finely chopped	4 oz
60 g	button mushrooms, chopped	2 oz
1 tsp	chopped fresh marjoram, or ¼ tsp dried marjoram	1 tsp
4 tbsp	grated horseradish	4 tbsp
30 g	cashew nuts, coarsely chopped	1 oz
¼ tsp	salt	¼ tsp
	freshly ground black pepper	
	celery leaves, for garnish	

Peel the onions, trimming off the root ends, but leaving the tops intact. Place them in a large saucepan of simmering water and cook them until they are soft but still keep their shape — about 10 minutes. Drain and cool. Slice lids off the pointed ends, about a quarter of the way down each onion. Push out the centres of the onions with a teaspoon, leaving shells about two layers thick. (Save the centres for a soup or stock.)

Preheat the oven to 180°C (350°F or Mark 4). Lightly brush a non-stick frying pan with oil and heat it over high heat. Add the lamb, stirring until it changes colour — about 2 minutes. Add the celeriac, mushrooms and marjoram, reduce the heat to medium, and cook for a further 2 minutes. Stir in the horseradish, cashew nuts, salt and some pepper and remove the pan from the heat.

Place the onion shells in a shallow ovenproof dish. Using a teaspoon, pack the lamb mixture as tightly as possible into the shells, piling it up above the shells if necessary. Place the lids beside the onions, cover the dish with aluminium foil and bake the onions until they are tender — about 40 minutes. Replace the lids and serve the onions garnished with celery leaves.

Spinach-Wrapped Cutlets Stuffed with Shiitake Mushrooms

Serves 6
Working time: about 50 minutes
Total time: about 1 hour and 30 minutes (includes soaking)

Calories **340**
Protein **29g**
Cholesterol **75mg**
Total fat **14g**
Saturated fat **5g**
Sodium **355mg**

12	best end of neck cutlets (about 90 g/3 oz each)	12
12	large spinach leaves, washed	12
24	shiitake mushrooms, soaked for 20 minutes in 30 cl (½ pint) of warm water	24
4 tsp	safflower oil	4 tsp
4 cm	piece fresh ginger root, julienned	1½ inch
12	shallots, eight finely sliced, four finely chopped	12
½ tsp	salt	½ tsp
	freshly ground black pepper	
4 tbsp	dry sherry	4 tbsp
½ litre	unsalted brown or chicken stock (recipes, page 137)	16 fl oz

Blanch the spinach leaves in boiling water for 2 to 3 seconds. Rinse them immediately in cold water and leave them to drain on tea towels.

Squeeze the shiitake mushrooms dry. Strain the soaking liquid through a muslin-lined sieve and reserve it. Reserve the 12 best looking mushrooms for garnish. Remove the stalks from the remaining mushrooms and finely slice the caps; keep the stalks and the sliced caps separate.

Put the oil in a heavy frying pan over low heat and sauté the ginger and the sliced shallots for 3 minutes. Add the sliced shiitake mushrooms and continue to fry for a further 5 minutes. Season the mushroom mixture with ⅛ teaspoon of the salt and some black pepper, and leave to cool while preparing the cutlets.

Trim the cutlets of all fat and loose bones, so that you are left with an eye of meat attached to a long rib bone. Using a small, sharp knife, scrape the rib bones clean of flesh and fat. Lay the cutlets flat on a work surface and make a horizontal slit in the side of each cutlet to form pockets about 2.5 cm (1 inch) deep by 2.5 cm (1 inch) wide for the mushroom stuffing.

Season the trimmed cutlets with ⅛ teaspoon of the salt and a little black pepper. Place a spinach leaf vein side up on the work surface and pare away a thin slice of the centre rib of the leaf, taking care not to cut through it. Divide the mushroom stuffing into 12 portions. Spoon half of one portion in the centre of the leaf; push the remaining half portion of stuffing into the pocket of a cutlet. Place the cutlet on the stuffing in the centre of the leaf so that the rib bone protrudes beyond the edge of the leaf. Wrap the ends of the leaf over the cutlet to enclose it, then fold over any loose edges to make a neat parcel. Fill and wrap the remaining cutlets in the same way, then set aside.

To make a sauce, put the chopped shallots and the sherry in a small saucepan, cover and simmer for 5 minutes. Add the stock and the reserved mushroom soaking liquid, return the mixture to the boil, add the reserved whole mushrooms and the stalks and simmer for 10 minutes. Remove the whole mushrooms with a slotted spoon and keep them warm. Increase the heat and boil the sauce until only 30 cl (½ pint) of liquid remains. Strain the sauce, season it with the remaining salt and keep it warm.

Meanwhile, pour enough water into a saucepan to fill it 2.5 cm (1 inch) deep. Set a steamer in the pan and bring the water to the boil. Place the cutlet parcels, seam side down, in the steamer, cover the pan tightly and steam them for 8 to 10 minutes.

Place two cutlet parcels on each of six warmed plates, surround them with sauce and garnish them with the whole mushrooms.

SUGGESTED ACCOMPANIMENT: *grilled sweet pepper strips tossed with sesame oil and toasted sesame seeds.*

Lamb and Leek Parcels

Serves 4
Working time: about 45 minutes
Total time: about 1 hour

Calories **215**
Protein **30g**
Cholesterol **75mg**
Total fat **9g**
Saturated fat **4g**
Sodium **265mg**

500 g	lean lamb (from the loin), trimmed of fat	1 lb
1	lime, juice and grated rind	1
1 tsp	virgin olive oil	1 tsp
1 tbsp	chopped fresh oregano	1 tbsp
½ tsp	salt	½ tsp
	freshly ground black pepper	
4	leeks, trimmed and the tough outer layers discarded	4
30 cl	unsalted chicken stock (recipe, page 137)	½ pint

Cut the lamb into 12 strips, each about 12.5 cm (5 inches) long by 1 cm (½ inch) wide. Put the meat into a small bowl together with the lime juice and rind, the olive oil, two thirds of the oregano, ¼ teaspoon of the salt and some black pepper. Stir the strips to coat them evenly and leave them to marinate at room temperature while you prepare the leeks.

Make a slit down the length of the three outer layers of each leek and remove these layers. Slice the leeks into rounds, wash them well and put them into a fire-proof casserole; set aside. Thoroughly wash the detached leek layers and cook them in boiling water until they are tender — 3 to 5 minutes. Refresh them in cold water and spread them on a tea towel to dry.

Preheat the oven to 230°C (450°F or Mark 8). Cut four of the cooked leek layers in half lengthwise. Spread one of the intact layers flat on a work surface. Lift a strip of lamb out of the marinade and lay it along the centre of the layer. Cover the lamb with one of the half leek layers, place a second strip of lamb on top, then another half layer and finally a third strip of lamb. Bring up the sides of the whole leek layer, place another whole leek layer on top and fold down its sides to form a neat open-ended parcel. Make up three more parcels in the same way. Reserve the marinade.

Place the lamb and leek parcels on top of the sliced leeks in the casserole. Add the chicken stock and the marinade, cover with aluminium foil and bake the parcels for 10 to 12 minutes for rare to medium meat.

Turn off the oven and transfer the leek parcels to a chopping board. Remove the leek slices from the casserole with a slotted spoon and put them in a warm serving dish. Cut each parcel into three pieces, and place them on top of the leek slices. Put the serving dish in the oven to keep warm.

Set the casserole over high heat and boil the cooking juices until only 15 cl (¼ pint) of liquid remains — about 2 minutes. Add the remaining oregano and salt and some black pepper. Pour the sauce over the leek parcels and serve immediately.

SUGGESTED ACCOMPANIMENTS: *grilled tomatoes stuffed with breadcrumbs and garlic; potato purée.*

Add the meat to the vegetables and stir in half of the Parmesan cheese, the salt and a generous grinding of pepper. Set the stuffing aside.

Remove the squash from the baking dish and discard the cooking water. Place the squash upside down on a towel to drain. When they are cool enough to handle, scoop out the flesh with a spoon, forming shells with walls approximately 5 mm (¼ inch) thick. Add the squash flesh to the lamb stuffing and stir to mix it in thoroughly.

Divide the stuffing between the four squash shells. Sprinkle a little of the remaining Parmesan cheese on top of each squash. Return the squash to the baking dish and bake them until they are hot — about 30 minutes. Serve the stuffed squash immediately.

SUGGESTED ACCOMPANIMENTS: *green salad; crusty rolls.*

Acorn Squash with Lamb and Vegetable Stuffing

Serves 4
Working time: about 1 hour
Total time: about 2 hours and 15 minutes

Calories **325**
Protein **26g**
Cholesterol **70mg**
Total fat **11g**
Saturated fat **4g**
Sodium **315mg**

500 g	lean lamb (from the leg or loin), trimmed of fat and minced (page 43)	1 lb
4	acorn squash (about 500 g/1 lb each)	4
1 tsp	safflower oil	1 tsp
75 g	French beans, trimmed and cut into 5 mm (¼ inch) pieces	2½ oz
90 g	fresh sweetcorn kernels (cut from one small cob) or frozen sweetcorn kernels, thawed	3 oz
1	onion, chopped	1
30 g	Parmesan cheese, freshly grated	1 oz
¼ tsp	salt	¼ tsp
	freshly ground black pepper	

Preheat the oven to 200°C (400°F or Mark 6).

Cut a 1 cm (½ inch) thick slice from the bottom of each acorn squash so that it will stand upright. Cut a 2.5 cm (1 inch) thick slice from the stem end of each squash and scoop out the seeds with a spoon. Set the squash, stem sides down, in a baking dish. Pour about ¼ litre (8 fl oz) of water into the dish, then cover it tightly with aluminium foil. Bake the squash until they are tender when pierced with the tip of a sharp knife — about 1 hour.

While the squash are baking, make the lamb and vegetable stuffing. Heat the oil in a large non-stick sauté pan over medium-high heat. Add the beans, sweetcorn and onion, and sauté them until the onion is soft and lightly browned — about 5 minutes. Transfer the vegetables to a large bowl. Increase the heat under the pan to high; add the lamb, and cook it, stirring and breaking it up with a wooden spoon, until it is evenly browned — about 5 minutes. Pour off any fat.

Patterning Sauces

1 POURING THE SAUCES. *Prepare two sauces of contrasting colour. Just before serving, pour some of one sauce into the centre of a flat-bottomed dining plate. Tip and swirl the plate to cover the bottom evenly. Carefully spoon some of the contrasting sauce on to the first sauce (above); move your hand to elongate the shape slightly.*

2 FEATHERING THE SAUCES. *Place the tip of a fine skewer in the contrasting sauce and draw it through the first sauce and back into the contrasting sauce to create a loop. Repeat the process to form a feathered pattern.*

Lamb Stuffed with a Chicken and Wild Mushroom Mousse

Serves 4
Working time: about 1 hour
Total time: about 2 hours (includes chilling)

Calories **400**	1	rack of lamb (500 g/1 lb), boned, the fatty flap of meat that extends from the eye removed	1
Protein **40g**			
Cholesterol **105mg**			
Total fat **15g**	⅛ tsp	salt	⅛ tsp
Saturated fat **7g**		freshly ground black pepper	
Sodium **235mg**	7 g	unsalted butter	¼ oz
	4	cherry tomatoes	4
		sprigs of parsley, for garnish	

Chicken and cep mousse		
10 g	dried ceps	⅓ oz
125 g	breast of chicken, cut into chunks, and chilled for at least 40 minutes	4 oz
1	egg white, chilled for at least 40 minutes	1
⅛ tsp	salt	⅛ tsp
1 tbsp	thick Greek yogurt, chilled	1 tbsp
	freshly ground black pepper	
½ tsp	chopped flat-leaf parsley	½ tsp

Morel sauces		
24	small dried morels	24
¼ litre	unsalted chicken stock (recipe, page 137)	8 fl oz
2 tbsp	dry sherry	2 tbsp
½ tsp	cornflour	½ tsp
3 tbsp	plain low-fat yogurt	3 tbsp

Put the ceps for the mousse and the morels for the sauce into a bowl together and cover them with 30 cl (½ pint) of lukewarm water. Set the bowl aside for 20 minutes while preparing the meat.

Remove any tough membrane left on the lamb, then make a horizontal slit lengthwise, cutting from the thinner edge, about three quarters of the way through the meat. Open it like a book and flatten it between two sheets of plastic film with a mallet or rolling-pin to an even thickness of about 5 mm (¼ inch). Season with the salt and some pepper and chill it in the refrigerator, still in the plastic film, while preparing the mousse.

Strain the mushroom soaking liquid through muslin; reserve the morels and the soaking liquid. Squeeze the ceps dry, rinse them in cold water to remove any grit, then squeeze them dry again and chop them finely. Set them aside.

To make the mousse, put the chicken into a chilled food processor with the egg white and salt. Process the chicken until it forms a smooth paste — 1 to 2 minutes. Press the mixture through a nylon sieve into a chilled clean bowl to remove any sinew. Beat the yogurt into the chicken paste, then add the chopped ceps, some pepper and the parsley, stirring gently until they are evenly distributed. Cover and chill the mousse in the refrigerator for at least 30 minutes.

Preheat the oven to 170°C (325°F or Mark 3). Unwrap the flattened lamb and spoon the chilled mousse along its centre in a sausage shape. Wrap the meat round the mousse, overlapping the two long edges by about 2.5 cm (1 inch). Tie the rolled meat in three or four places with string. Melt the butter in a heavy frying pan and brown the meat evenly over medium heat, then wrap it in a sheet of aluminium foil and bake it in the oven for 15 minutes. Turn off the oven, remove the meat, and pour off and reserve the juices collected in the foil. Cover the meat loosely with the foil again and return it to the oven for 10 minutes before slicing. Place the cherry tomatoes in the oven to warm them through and loosen their skins.

To make the sauce, put the stock, sherry and reserved mushroom soaking liquid into a saucepan. Boil gently until only half the liquid remains. Add the morels and poach them for 10 minutes, then remove them with a slotted spoon and keep them warm. Add the reserved meat juice to the sauce. Blend the cornflour with a tablespoon of water and stir it into the pan. Bring the sauce back to the boil, turn the heat down and simmer for 2 to 3 minutes, stirring constantly until it thickens and clears. Place the yogurt in a bowl over a pan of simmering water to warm it through. Blend one third of the sauce into the yogurt and whisk until it is smooth. Keep the plain sauce and the yogurt sauce warm in separate containers.

Carefully peel the cherry tomatoes. To serve, cut the stuffed lamb diagonally into 16 slices with a sharp knife. Pour a quarter of the plain sauce to one side of each of four warmed plates, then a quarter of the yogurt sauce on top. Feather the edge of the yogurt sauce with a skewer, as shown on the opposite page. Arrange four slices of meat on the edge of the sauce and garnish with parsley sprigs, the cherry tomatoes and the morels.

SUGGESTED ACCOMPANIMENT: *French beans.*

Roast Five-Spice Leg of Lamb

"FIVE-SPICE" IS A TRADITIONAL CHINESE SEASONING. THE
ACTUAL SPICES USED TO MAKE IT UP VARY FROM REGION TO
REGION, BUT THREE OF THEM ARE ALWAYS PRESENT; CASSIA
BARK (CHINESE CINNAMON), STAR ANISE AND SICHUAN PEPPER.

Serves 8
Working time: about 45 minutes
Total time: about 16 hours (includes marinating)

Calories **225**
Protein **32g**
Cholesterol **75mg**
Total fat **9g**
Saturated fat **4g**
Sodium **140mg**

1.5 kg	half leg of lamb, shank end, trimmed of fat	3 lb
1 tbsp	quince or apple jelly	1 tbsp
600 g	small carrots	1¼ lb
600 g	pickling onions, peeled	1¼ lb
½ tsp	arrowroot	½ tsp
"Five-spice" marinade		
20 g	cassia bark (Chinese cinnamon)	¾ oz
20 g	star anise	¾ oz
15 g	liquorice root	½ oz
12	cloves	12
1½ tsp	Sichuan peppercorns	1½ tsp
½	dried tangerine peel, or three strips fresh orange rind	½
1 or 2	dried chili peppers (caution, page 83)	1 or 2
6 cl	dark soy sauce or shoyu	2 fl oz
6 cl	light soy sauce	2 fl oz
½ litre	Chinese rice wine or dry sherry	16 fl oz
2 tsp	brown sugar	2 tsp
4	garlic cloves, unpeeled	4
2.5 cm	piece fresh ginger root, unpeeled and cut into quarters	1 inch

To make the marinade, put the cassia bark, star anise, liquorice root, cloves, Sichuan peppercorns, tangerine peel and chili pepper in a small piece of muslin and tie it up with cotton string, leaving one long end. Mix the dark and the light soy sauce, the rice wine and the sugar with ½ litre (16 fl oz) of water in a large saucepan. Bring the liquid to a simmer, stirring to dissolve the sugar, then add the garlic, ginger and the spice bag, tying its string to the handle of the pan. Cover the pan and let the marinade simmer for 30 minutes, skimming off any scum from time to time.

At the end of this period, add the leg of lamb and boil it, uncovered, for 6 to 7 minutes, turning it once. Reduce the heat to very low and skim the marinade, then cover the pan and simmer the lamb for 30 minutes. Turn the meat after 15 minutes and skim again if necessary. Let the lamb cool in the liquid, then marinate it in the refrigerator for 12 to 24 hours, turning it several times.

Preheat the oven to 230°C (450°F or Mark 8). Remove the leg from the pan, reserving half of the marinade for basting and deglazing, and the other half for the sauce. Place the meat on a rack over a roasting pan and roast it for 10 minutes. Reduce the heat to 180°C (350°F or Mark 4), put a pan of cold water on the bottom shelf, and continue cooking for 1 hour to 1 hour and 20 minutes, for medium to well-done meat respectively; baste the meat several times with the marinade. Ten minutes before the end of roasting time, glaze the meat: mix the quince or apple jelly with 1 teaspoon of boiling water, brush this solution over the leg, and return it to the oven.

While the lamb is roasting, begin to make the sauce. Strain the remaining half of the marinade into a saucepan through a fine sieve, bring it to the boil and add the carrots. Let the liquid return to the boil, reduce the heat and simmer the carrots for 5 minutes, then add the onions and simmer the vegetables until they are tender — about 15 minutes. Remove the pan from the heat and leave the vegetables in the liquid for 10 minutes to absorb its colour. Remove them with a slotted spoon and keep them warm. Strain the liquid into a saucepan and set it aside.

When the meat is cooked, turn off the oven and transfer the leg to a large platter. Leave it to rest for 15 minutes in the oven with the door slightly ajar. Meanwhile, skim off any fat from the roasting pan, put the pan over a high heat and add about 3 tablespoons of the marinade. Stir the liquid as it comes to the boil, scraping off any deposits from the base of the pan. Strain the pan juices and add them to the vegetable cooking liquid. Boil the liquid rapidly for 1 to 2 minutes. Add 15 cl (¼ pint) of water. Mix the arrowroot with 1 tablespoon of water and add it to the sauce. Return it to the boil and cook until the sauce thickens and clears — 2 to 3 minutes. Pour it into a serving bowl.

Arrange the vegetables round the lamb joint and carve at the table.

SUGGESTED ACCOMPANIMENTS: *boiled rice; quince jelly.*

EDITOR'S NOTE: *All the spices required for this recipe can be purchased in Chinese grocery shops. Dried tangerine peel, sometimes labelled "orange peel", is usually sold in small plastic bags with the peel broken into four pieces.*

Parslied Leg of Lamb Baked in Dough

IN THIS RECIPE, A PASTE OF FLOUR AND WATER WORKS LIKE A CLAY OVEN, SEALING IN THE FLAVOURS AND KEEPING THE MEAT MOIST AND TENDER.

Serves 10
Working time: about 30 minutes
Total time: about 2 hours and 30 minutes

Calories **210**
Protein **30g**
Cholesterol **80mg**
Total fat **10g**
Saturated fat **4g**
Sodium **185mg**

2.5 kg	leg of lamb, trimmed of fat	5 lb
6	garlic cloves	6
¾ tsp	salt	¾ tsp
	freshly ground black pepper	
4 tbsp	chopped parsley	4 tbsp
1 tbsp	virgin olive oil	1 tbsp
750 g	plain flour	1 ½ lb

Preheat the oven to 200°C (400°F or Mark 6).

Work the garlic cloves and salt into a creamy paste with a mortar and pestle. Mix in some freshly ground black pepper, the parsley and the olive oil. Rub this mixture evenly all over the leg of lamb.

Put the flour in a large mixing bowl and make a well in the centre. Add 45 cl (¾ pint) of cold water and mix to make a soft dough. Lightly knead the dough on a floured surface until it is smooth, then roll it out into a rectangle that is large enough to completely encase the leg of lamb.

Place the lamb upper side down in the centre of the dough. Bring the short sides of the rectangle up and over each end of the leg, then fold in the long edges to encase the lamb completely. Mould the dough neatly round the leg and press the dough edges well together to seal the casing.

Place the lamb in a large roasting pan with the joins in the dough underneath. Sprinkle the dough lightly with flour. Cook the lamb for 2 hours.

To serve, break open and discard the casing, by now baked to hardness, then carve the leg of lamb in the normal way.

SUGGESTED ACCOMPANIMENTS: *braised leeks; glazed carrots; creamed potatoes.*

4 Neat vine leaf packages, stuffed with spiced minced lamb and rice, need only half the traditional cooking time when prepared in a microwave oven (recipe, opposite

Microwaving Lamb

Quick, clean and inexpensive to run, a microwave oven offers undoubted convenience. For lamb cookery it is also versatile, as demonstrated in the following recipes which range from a traditional cottage pie *(page 132)* to satisfy robust appetites, to lamb timbales *(page 124)* that will gladden the eye as well as the palate of the most sophisticated diner.

To get the best results from your microwave oven, you should understand its strengths. Because microwaves penetrate only about 5 cm (2 inches) into the food, it is ideal for dishes where the meat is diced or cut into strips. To ensure that the meat cooks evenly, simply stir it from time to time. Recipes for minced lamb are also very successful; the meat loaf on page 129 requires only 10 to 12 minutes in the oven.

But large cuts that are generally roasted can also be cooked successfully in a microwave oven, provided they are turned and repositioned on the roasting dish half way through the cooking period. The 2 kg (4 lb) boned leg of lamb on page 127 cooks in just over half an hour; a roasting bag helps to seal in the moisture and preserve the meat's natural succulence. Never salt cuts of lamb before microwaving them; salting tends to dry out and toughen the meat.

A crucial element in microwave cookery is the "standing time" — a period after the food has been removed from the oven but continues to cook. This can account for up to half of the total cooking time. Test for doneness only at the end of standing time. With a roast, testing is simplified by using a meat thermometer inserted into the thickest part.

The power at which you microwave lamb depends upon the quality of the meat. Tender cuts — including minced meat — are best cooked on high (100 per cent power). Less tender cuts should be covered and cooked in liquid on medium (50 per cent power). When cooking a dish covered with plastic film, remember to pull back one corner so that steam can escape.

Microwave cookery does not brown meat, but often other ingredients compensate; lamb baked in saffron yogurt *(page 127)*, for instance, assumes the vivid colour of its sauce. A few of the recipes, however, call for a browning dish — a dish specifically designed to give meat cooked in the microwave oven the seared and browned surface normally associated with roasting, grilling or frying.

Stuffed Vine Leaves

Serves 6
Working (and total) time: about 1 hour

Calories **190**
Protein **16g**
Cholesterol **35mg**
Total fat **8g**
Saturated fat **3g**
Sodium **50mg**

250 g	lean lamb (from the leg or loin), trimmed of fat and minced (page 43)	8 oz
60 g	brown rice	2 oz
30	fresh vine leaves, or preserved vine leaves rinsed under cold running water	30
1	small onion, finely chopped	1
30 g	pine-nuts	1 oz
30 g	currants	1 oz
1 tsp	ground cinnamon	1 tsp
1 tsp	ground allspice	1 tsp
2½ tbsp	fresh lemon juice	2½ tbsp
	freshly ground black pepper	
1	egg white, lightly beaten	1
6	garlic cloves, thinly sliced	6
30 cl	puréed tomatoes	½ pint
1 tsp	soft brown sugar	1 tsp
6 tbsp	plain low-fat yogurt, for garnish	6 tbsp

Put the rice in a bowl with 20 cl (7 fl oz) of boiling water. Cover the bowl loosely and microwave on high for 5 minutes. Reduce the power to medium and cook for 5 minutes more. Let the rice stand for 5 minutes, then drain off any liquid and leave it to cool.

If you are using fresh vine leaves, put them in a bowl and cover them with water. Microwave on high until the water boils — about 5 minutes. Leave to stand for 10 minutes, drain and trim off the stalks.

Mix the lamb, rice, onion, pine-nuts, currants, cinnamon, allspice, 1 teaspoon of the lemon juice and some pepper together in a bowl. Mix in the egg white.

Lay a vine leaf, vein side up, on the work surface. Place a heaped teaspoon of the filling near the base of the leaf and fold the sides towards the centre. Roll up the leaf into a cigar shape. Stuff the other leaves in the same way. Place them seam side down in a baking dish and tuck the slivers of garlic between them.

Mix together the tomatoes, the remaining lemon juice, the sugar and some pepper and pour the mixture over the leaves. Cover with plastic film, leaving a corner open. Microwave on high for 10 minutes. Reduce the power to medium and cook for another 15 minutes. Allow the stuffed vine leaves to stand for 5 minutes, then serve them with the yogurt.

SUGGESTED ACCOMPANIMENT: *salad of tomatoes, cucumber, peppers, onion and olives.*

Lamb Timbales

THIS RECIPE IS IDEAL FOR USING A FILLET LEFT OVER FROM
BONING A LOIN FOR DISHES THAT CALL FOR THE EYE ONLY.

Serves 6
Working (and total) time: about 1 hour and 15 minutes

Calories **150**
Protein **17g**
Cholesterol **40mg**
Total fat **7g**
Saturated fat **3g**
Sodium **145mg**

175 g	lean loin, all fat and connective tissue removed, triple-minced and well chilled	6 oz
125 g	lamb slices from the fillet end of leg, trimmed of fat and flattened (page 24)	4 oz
1	large sweet red pepper	1
3	courgettes (about 300 g/10½ oz), ends trimmed	3
30 g	fresh fine breadcrumbs	1 oz
4 tbsp	skimmed milk	4 tbsp
1 tsp	arrowroot	1 tsp
6 tbsp	thick Greek yogurt	6 tbsp
1 tsp	finely chopped fresh marjoram, or ¼ tsp dried marjoram	1 tsp
1 tbsp	tomato paste	1 tbsp
½ tsp	salt	½ tsp
¼ tsp	white pepper	¼ tsp
1 tsp	virgin olive oil	1 tsp

Prick the pepper several times with a fork or skewer, place it on a double layer of paper towels and microwave it on high for 5 minutes, until it is soft, turning it once. Place the pepper in a bowl and cover it with plastic film. After 5 to 10 minutes, skin, halve, seed and derib the pepper. Using a 4 cm (1½ inch) diameter biscuit cutter, stamp out six rounds from the pepper and set them aside.

Cut two thin slices from one end of each courgette, then cut the courgettes into thin strips by running the full width of a potato peeler along their length. Place the slices and strips in a shallow dish, add 2 tablespoons of water and cover with plastic film, leaving a corner open. Microwave on high for 2 minutes, carefully turning the slices and strips with a slotted spatula after 1 minute. Lay the softened slices and strips on double paper towels and leave them to drain.

Place a courgette slice, followed by a pepper round, in the base of each cup of a six-cup microwave muffin tray — the cups used here are 6 by 4.5 cm (2½ by 1 ¾ inches) — then line the cups with slightly overlapping courgette strips. Allow 4 cm (1½ inches) of each courgette strip to hang over the rim of the cup. Set the lined cups aside.

To make a mousse, soak the breadcrumbs in the milk for 2 minutes. In a small bowl, blend the arrowroot with 1 tablespoon of the yogurt, then stir in the remaining yogurt. In a large bowl, combine the minced lamb and soaked breadcrumbs, then stir in the yogurt, marjoram, tomato paste, salt and some pepper. Place all the ingredients in a food processor and process until smooth — about 2 minutes. Spoon half of the lamb mousse mixture into the cups to half fill them.

Preheat a browning dish according to the manufacturer's instructions. Using a 5.5 cm (2¼ inch) plain cutter as a guide, cut six rounds from the escalopes using a small, sharp knife. Pour the oil into the browning dish and immediately arrange the rounds of meat in the dish in a single layer. Microwave on high for 1 minute until brown, turning the escalopes once after 30 seconds. Remove them from the oven and gently place one on top of the mousse mixture in each cup. Distribute the remaining mousse among the cups — it will mound up a little above the rims. Fold the courgette strip ends over the mousse to enclose it.

Cover the cups loosely with plastic film and cook the timbales on medium high for 4 minutes, turning them once. Remove them from the oven and allow them to rest, still covered, for a further 4 minutes. Turn the timbales out on to individual plates, and serve hot.

SUGGESTED ACCOMPANIMENTS: *tomato concassée; green salad.*

EDITOR'S NOTE: *For a smooth mousse, it is essential to mince the meat in this recipe by passing it through a mincer three times; a food processor will not remove the connective tissue.*

Sage-Marinated Lamb Chops

Serves 4
Working time: about 25 minutes
Total time: about 1 hour and 30 minutes (includes marinating)

Calories **235**
Protein **25g**
Cholesterol **75mg**
Total fat **12g**
Saturated fat **6g**
Sodium **175mg**

8	loin chops (about 125g/4 oz each), trimmed of fat	8
2 tsp	chopped fresh sage, or ¾ tsp dried sage, crumbled	2 tsp
3	garlic cloves, finely chopped	3
1	lemon, grated rind only	1
2 tbsp	balsamic vinegar, or 1½ tbsp red wine vinegar mixed with ½ tsp honey	2 tbsp
1 tbsp	dark brown sugar	1 tbsp
1 tbsp	brandy	1 tbsp
¼ tsp	salt	¼ tsp
	freshly ground black pepper	

Mix the sage, garlic, lemon rind, vinegar, brown sugar, brandy, salt and some pepper in a 20 cm (8 inch) square glass dish. Add the lamb chops to the dish and turn to coat them with the marinade. Let the lamb chops stand for 1 hour at room temperature, turning them every 15 minutes.

Microwave the chops, uncovered, on high for 2 minutes. Turn the chops over, rearranging them so that the chops that were at the outside of the dish are now at the centre. Cook the chops on high for 3 minutes more. Remove the dish from the oven and cover it loosely with foil. Let the lamb chops stand for 5 minutes before serving them.

SUGGESTED ACCOMPANIMENTS: *stewed tomatoes; steamed new potatoes.*

Lamb Roast with Winter Vegetables

Serves 8
Working time: about 30 minutes
Total time: about 1 hour

Calories **220**
Protein **26g**
Cholesterol **75mg**
Total fat **8g**
Saturated fat **3g**
Sodium **175mg**

2 kg	leg of lamb, fillet end, trimmed of fat and boned	4 lb
2 tsp	chili powder	2 tsp
1 tbsp	chopped fresh rosemary, or 2 tsp dried rosemary, crumbled	1 tbsp
	freshly ground black pepper	
1	small cauliflower (about 600 g/1 ¼ lb), trimmed and divided into florets	1
3	carrots, sliced on the diagonal into 2.5 cm (1 inch) pieces	3
500 g	Brussels sprouts, trimmed	1 lb
15 cl	unsalted brown or chicken stock (recipes, page 137)	¼ pint
¼ tsp	salt	¼ tsp
1 tbsp	cornflour, mixed with 2 tbsp water	1 tbsp

With your fingers, rub the chili powder over the outside of the joint, then sprinkle it with the rosemary and a generous grinding of pepper. Place the lamb in a roasting bag and tie the bag loosely with string or a strip of plastic film, leaving an opening for steam to escape. Make sure that the opening faces upwards so that the cooking juices do not run out. Place the lamb in a shallow dish.

Microwave the lamb on medium high for 16 minutes. Turn the lamb over, taking care to keep the juices in the bag; cook the lamb for 16 minutes more for medium-rare meat.

Remove the lamb from the oven and take it out of the roasting bag. Let the roast stand for 10 minutes. Pour the juices that have collected in the bag into a large bowl. Set the bowl aside. (At this point an instant-reading meat thermometer inserted into the centre of the roast should register 77°C/170°F; if it does not, cook the lamb for another 5 minutes on medium.)

While the roast is resting, pour enough water into a large saucepan to fill it about 2.5 cm (1 inch) deep. Put a vegetable steamer in the pan and bring the water to the boil. Put the cauliflower, carrots and Brussels sprouts into the steamer, cover tightly and steam the vegetables until tender — about 10 minutes.

To make the sauce, skim the fat off the top of the meat juices. Stir the stock, salt and cornflour mixture into the juices and microwave the sauce on high until it has thickened — about 2 minutes. Stir again.

Slice the meat. Arrange it on a platter surrounded by the vegetables and pour the sauce over all.

SUGGESTED ACCOMPANIMENT: *wholemeal bread rolls.*

Lamb Baked in Saffron Yogurt

Serves 4
Working time: about 30 minutes
Total time: about 4 hours and 45 minutes
(includes marinating)

Calories **195**
Protein **25g**
Cholesterol **80mg**
Total fat **8g**
Saturated fat **3g**
Sodium **90mg**

600 g	lean lamb (from the leg or loin), trimmed of fat and cut into 2.5 cm (1 inch) cubes	1 ¼ lb
3	garlic cloves, finely chopped	3
2 tbsp	finely chopped fresh ginger root	2 tbsp
¼ tsp	saffron threads or turmeric	¼ tsp
1 tbsp	cornflour	1 tbsp
1	fresh hot green chili pepper, seeded, deribbed and finely chopped (caution, page 83)	1
17.5 cl	plain low-fat yogurt	6 fl oz
4	radishes, thinly sliced, for garnish	4
2	spring onions, trimmed and thinly sliced, for garnish	2

Put the lamb cubes, garlic, ginger, saffron or turmeric, cornflour, chili pepper and yogurt in a baking dish. Mix the ingredients well together, then cover the dish and refrigerate it for about 4 hours.

Microwave the lamb and its marinade, covered with greaseproof paper, on medium for 15 minutes, stirring the mixture every 5 minutes. Let the dish stand for 5 minutes; stir it once again before serving. Garnish the lamb with the radishes and spring onions.

SUGGESTED ACCOMPANIMENTS: *yellow rice; mixed salad.*

EDITOR'S NOTE: *Do not marinate the lamb cubes for more than six hours, otherwise they will become too soft.*

Chili Meatballs with Two Pepper Sauces

Serves 4
Working time: about 30 minutes
Total time: about 40 minutes

Calories **225**
Protein **25g**
Cholesterol **60mg**
Total fat **8g**
Saturated fat **3g**
Sodium **175mg**

350 g	lean lamb (from the leg or loin), trimmed of fat and minced (page 43)	12 oz
1	stick celery, finely chopped	1
60 g	fresh wholemeal breadcrumbs	2 oz
2	small hot chili peppers, finely chopped (caution, page 83)	2
2 tbsp	finely cut chives, plus a few chives for garnish	2 tbsp
1 tsp	anchovy essence	1 tsp
¼ tsp	salt	¼ tsp
1 tsp	virgin olive oil	1 tsp
Pepper sauces		
1	sweet red pepper	1
1	sweet yellow pepper	1
2 tsp	white wine vinegar	2 tsp
2 tbsp	thick Greek yogurt	2 tbsp

First make the sauces. Prick the sweet peppers in several places with a fork or skewer, place them, spaced well apart, on a double layer of paper towels in the microwave oven and cook them on high until they are soft — about 5 minutes — turning them once. Place the peppers in a bowl, cover with plastic film, and leave for 5 to 10 minutes. Skin and seed the pep-

pers. Roughly chop the red pepper and purée it in a blender or food processor with 1 teaspoon of the vinegar and 2 tablespoons of water until smooth. Transfer the purée to a small bowl and stir in 1 tablespoon of the yogurt. Process the yellow pepper in the same way, transfer it to a separate bowl and stir in the remaining yogurt.

To make the meatballs, mix together the lamb, celery, breadcrumbs, chilies, cut chives, anchovy essence and salt. Using your hands, form the mixture into 20 balls each about 2.5 cm (1 inch) in diameter.

Preheat a browning dish following the manufacturer's instructions. Immediately add the olive oil and meatballs, turning the meatballs until they stop sizzling. Cover them with a lid, or plastic film with a corner pulled back, and cook them on high for 5 minutes, turning once. Leave them to stand for 3 minutes.

Meanwhile, heat the sauces on medium for 1½ minutes; if the bowls are small enough, they should fit in the oven together. Spoon the red pepper sauce round the edge of four warmed serving plates, and spoon the yellow pepper sauce into the centre. Use a skewer to draw a pattern in the sauces (page 118).

Distribute the meatballs among the plates. Serve them immediately, garnished with the chives.

SUGGESTED ACCOMPANIMENT: pilaff rice.

Meat Loaf with Olives

Serves 6
Working time: about 15 minutes
Total time: about 30 minutes

Calories **275**
Protein **32g**
Cholesterol **85mg**
Total fat **12g**
Saturated fat **5g**
Sodium **320mg**

850 g	lean lamb (from the leg or loin), trimmed of fat and minced (page 43)	1 ¾ lb
1	egg white, lightly beaten	1
1 tbsp	chopped fresh oregano, or 1 tsp dried oregano	1 tbsp
¼ tsp	cayenne pepper	¼ tsp
2	garlic cloves, finely chopped	2
4 tbsp	finely chopped onion	4 tbsp
30 g	parsley, chopped	1 oz
6	oil-cured black olives, stoned and finely chopped	6
60 g	dry breadcrumbs	2 oz
4 tbsp	freshly grated Parmesan cheese	4 tbsp
1 tbsp	red wine vinegar	1 tbsp
1 ½ tbsp	tomato paste	1 ½ tbsp

In a large bowl, combine the egg white, oregano, cayenne pepper, garlic and onion. Add the lamb, parsley, olives, breadcrumbs, Parmesan cheese, vinegar and 1 tablespoon of the tomato paste. Using a wooden spoon, mix all the ingredients together until they are well combined.

Shape the meat mixture into a log about 7.5 cm (3 inches) in diameter. Place the log in a shallow baking dish and spread the remaining ½ tablespoon of tomato paste over the surface of the meat. Cook the loaf, un-covered, on high for 10 to 12 minutes, rotating the dish a half turn midway through the cooking time. Let the meat loaf stand for 10 minutes. To serve, cut the loaf into 12 slices.

SUGGESTED ACCOMPANIMENTS: *mashed swede; steamed shredded spring greens.*

Diced Lamb with Pink Grapefruit and Tarragon

Serves 4
Working time: about 30 minutes
Total time: about 45 minutes

500 g	lean lamb (from the leg or loin), trimmed of fat and cut into 1 cm (½ inch) cubes	1 lb
1½	pink grapefruits	1½
125 g	spring onions, trimmed and cut diagonally into 2.5 cm (1 inch) pieces	4 oz
3 tbsp	dry white vermouth	3 tbsp
1 tsp	chopped fresh tarragon, or 1 tbsp dried tarragon	1 tsp
750 g	spinach, washed, stems removed	1½ lb
2 tbsp	cornflour	2 tbsp
1 tsp	clear honey	1 tsp
¼ tsp	salt	¼ tsp
	freshly ground black pepper	
4 tbsp	crème fraîche	4 tbsp

Calories **340**
Protein **35g**
Cholesterol **75mg**
Total fat **11g**
Saturated fat **6g**
Sodium **310mg**

Squeeze out and reserve the juice from the half grapefruit. Using a sharp knife, remove and discard the skin and white pith from the remaining grapefruit, then carefully cut out the flesh from between the membranes and set the segments aside.

Put the lamb, grapefruit juice, spring onions, vermouth and tarragon in a 2.25 litre (4 pint) casserole dish and stir. Cover with a lid, or with plastic film pulled back at one corner, and microwave on medium for 15 minutes, stirring every 5 minutes. Remove the casserole from the oven and leave it to stand while you prepare the spinach.

Shake off any excess water from the spinach and put it in a large bowl. Cover the bowl with plastic film, pulling back one corner, and cook the spinach on high until it is wilted and tender — 5 to 6 minutes. Drain the spinach well, squeezing out as much water as possible, and chop it roughly. Arrange the spinach round the edge of a microwave-safe serving dish.

Blend the cornflour with 2 tablespoons of water and stir the mixture into the lamb, together with half of the grapefruit segments and the honey. Cook, uncovered, on high for 5 minutes, stirring twice during this time, then stir well once more. Season the lamb with the salt and some pepper, add the remaining grapefruit segments and stir in the *crème fraîche*. Spoon the lamb mixture into the centre of the spinach-rimmed dish and reheat on high for 2 minutes. Serve immediately.

SUGGESTED ACCOMPANIMENT: *boiled rice.*

Butterfly Chops with a Barbecue Sauce

BECAUSE METAL MUST NOT BE USED IN THE MICROWAVE OVEN, THE BONED CHOPS IN THIS RECIPE ARE SECURED WITH WOODEN COCKTAIL STICKS INSTEAD OF METAL SKEWERS.

Serves 6
Working (and total) time: about 45 minutes

Calories **270**
Protein **28g**
Cholesterol **80mg**
Total fat **12g**
Saturated fat **5g**
Sodium **280mg**

6	double loin butterfly chops (about 175 g/6 oz each), boned and trimmed of fat (page 32), secured with wooden cocktail sticks	6
	unpeeled pineapple wedges, for garnish	
Barbecue sauce		
250 g	fresh pineaple flesh, or unsweetened canned pineapple chunks, drained	8 oz
200 g	canned tomatoes, drained and sieved	7 oz
3 tbsp	low-sodium soy sauce or shoyu	3 tbsp
3 tbsp	clear honey	3 tbsp
2 tbsp	red wine vinegar	2 tbsp
2	garlic cloves, crushed	2
¼ tsp	cayenne pepper	¼ tsp
2 tsp	paprika	2 tsp
	freshly ground black pepper	

To make the sauce, purée the pineapple flesh in a blender or food processor, then press the purée through a nylon sieve into a large, clean bowl, to remove any stringy pieces. Add the remaining sauce ingredients to the pineapple purée and stir them in well. Cook the sauce, uncovered, on high for 10 minutes, stirring every 2 minutes. Set the sauce aside.

Heat a browning dish for the maximum time allowed in the instruction manual. Brown the chops on both sides in the dish, then cover and microwave on high for 3 minutes; turn and rearrange the chops after 1½ minutes. Skim off any fat.

Pour the barbecue sauce over and round the meat. Microwave, uncovered, for 4 minutes, turning and re-arranging the chops after 2 minutes. Serve the chops garnished with the pineapple wedges.

SUGGESTED ACCOMPANIMENTS: *jacket potatoes; green salad.*

Cottage Pie

Serves 6
Working (and total) time: about 1 hour and 30 minutes

Calories **250**
Protein **22g**
Cholesterol **55mg**
Total fat **8g**
Saturated fat **3g**
Sodium **240mg**

500 g	lean lamb from fillet end of leg, trimmed of fat and minced (page 43)	1 lb
500 g	potatoes, peeled and sliced	1 lb
250 g	carrots, peeled and sliced	8 oz
250 g	swede, peeled and sliced	8 oz
1 tbsp	safflower oil	1 tbsp
1	large onion, halved and thinly sliced	1
20 g	plain flour	¾ oz
15 cl	unsalted veal stock (recipe, page 137)	¼ pint
	freshly ground black pepper	
½ tsp	salt	½ tsp
2 tbsp	chopped parsley	2 tbsp

Put the potatoes, carrots, and swede into a large microwave-safe mixing bowl with 6 tablespoons of cold water. Cover the bowl with plastic film, leaving a corner open. Microwave on high, stirring every 5 minutes, until the vegetables are softened — about 20 minutes in total. Remove the bowl from the oven and allow the vegetables to stand for 5 minutes.

Meanwhile, heat a browning dish on high for the maximum time allowed in the manufacturer's instructions. Add the oil and the onion. Cover and microwave on high for 2 to 3 minutes, until the onion is softened. Add the minced lamb and cook, uncovered, on high for 2 minutes, stirring every 30 seconds with a fork to break up the meat. Stir in the flour and add the stock. Microwave on high for 3 minutes, stirring every minute. Season with some black pepper and half of the salt; stir in the parsley. Spoon the meat into a microwave-safe serving dish.

Using a vegetable masher, mash the potatoes, carrots and swede together with any liquid left in the bowl, to produce a creamy purée. Season with some black pepper and the remaining salt. Spoon the vegetable purée evenly over the meat and mark swirls on the surface of the purée with a small palette knife.

Microwave the cottage pie on high for 15 minutes, giving the dish a quarter turn every 5 minutes. Serve the pie immediately.

SUGGESTED ACCOMPANIMENT: *steamed broccoli or spinach.*

Mediterranean Courgettes

Serves 4

Working (and total) time: about 30 minutes

Calories **160**
Protein **20g**
Cholesterol **50mg**
Total fat **5g**
Saturated fat **2g**
Sodium **240mg**

250 g	lean lamb (from the leg or loin), trimmed of fat and minced (page 43)	8 oz
4	courgettes (about 100 g/3½ oz) each, ends trimmed	4
1 tsp	virgin olive oil	1 tsp
½	garlic clove	½
30 g	sun-dried tomatoes, drained of any oil and chopped	1 oz
1 tbsp	tomato paste	1 tbsp
½ tsp	ground cinnamon	½ tsp
30 g	raisins	1 oz
15 g	pine-nuts	½ oz
1 ½ tsp	balsamic vinegar	1 ½ tsp
2 tbsp	finely chopped fresh basil, or 2 tsp dried basil	2 tbsp
½ tsp	salt	½ tsp
¼ tsp	freshly ground black pepper	¼ tsp

Halve the courgettes lengthwise and arrange them in a single layer in a shallow dish, cut side upwards. Add 1 tablespoon of water and cover the dish with plastic film, pulling back one corner. Cook the courgettes on high for 8 minutes; half way through the cooking time, rearrange them and move the inside pieces to the edge of the dish. Drain the courgettes well. Scoop out the pulp, taking care to leave the skins intact, and place the pulp in a sieve to drain.

Put the oil into a shallow dish and heat it on high for 15 seconds. Spear the garlic on a fork and wipe it round the hot dish to infuse the oil. Discard the garlic. Break up the minced lamb with a fork and add it to the dish, together with the sun-dried tomato, tomato paste and cinnamon. Cook on high until no pink meat is visible — 3 to 4 minutes — stirring and breaking up the meat thoroughly with a fork after every minute. When the meat is cooked, drain off any residual fat.

Add the courgette pulp, raisins and pine-nuts to the meat, and stir in the vinegar, basil, salt and pepper. Pile the mixture into the courgette skins and arrange them in a singe layer in the shallow dish.

Cover the dish with plastic film, leaving one corner open. Cook the stuffed courgettes on high until they are tender — 4 to 6 minutes, rearranging them half way through the cooking time. Leave the courgettes to stand, covered, for 2 minutes before serving them.

SUGGESTED ACCOMPANIMENTS: *rocket and radicchio salad; puréed potatoes.*

EDITOR'S NOTE: *For this dish, tender young courgettes are needed. If you can only obtain mature courgettes, precook them whole in boiling water containing 1 teaspoon of salt for 2 minutes to remove any bitterness in the skins.*

Techniques

Boning a Loin of Lamb

1 REMOVING THE FATTY FLAP. A loin is usually sold with a flap of fatty meat attached to it. Cut off the flap where it joins the loin. Discard the flap.

2 STARTING THE BONING. With the fatty layer of the loin facing down, insert the tip of a sharp, pointed knife between the meat and the backbone, and use short, slicing strokes to separate them.

3 REMOVING THE FILLET. Carefully pulling away the meat with one hand, continue cutting along the ribs until the fillet is freed.

4 REMOVING THE EYE. Flip the rib bones over to expose the underneath. Again, carefully cut the meat from the bones, using the same technique as demonstrated in Steps 2 and 3.

5 PEELING OFF THE FATTY LAYER. Pick up the eye in your hands and remove the thick, white layer of fat from the meat by gently pulling it off. If this is done carefully, the whole layer of fat should come away in one piece.

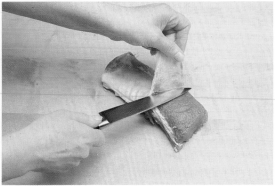

6 STRIPPING OFF THE SILVER SKIN. With the tip of the knife, cut under the whitish membrane of the eye to form a tab. Pull the tab taut, insert the knife under it and remove the silver skin.

Preparing a Loin Chop

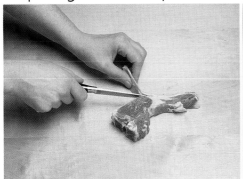 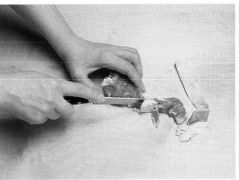 

1 *REMOVING THE SKIN. Place the chop on a wooden board. Insert the tip of a small, sharp knife in the small channel across the base of the bone and prise out the piece of white spinal cord. Then trim the skin and underlying fat from the convex side of the meat (above).*

2 *TRIMMING OFF EXCESS FAT. Carefully cut away most of the fat between the eye and the flap, leaving enough of the tissue to keep the chop in one piece.*

3 *SHAPING THE CHOP. Curl the flap around the fillet to form a neat shape. Insert a skewer or cocktail stick through the flap to keep it in place.*

Preparing Racks for Roasting

1 *STRIPPING OFF THE BARK. Remove any remnant of the shoulder blade, (page 136, Step 1). With the racks concave side up, carefully peel the bark — the outer membrane — away from the underlying fat and meat. Start at one corner, and when you have loosened enough bark, grasp it with one hand and firmly hold down the fat and meat with the other hand as you strip it off.*

2 *EXPOSING THE RIB ENDS. Score a straight line across the rack, about 5 cm (2 inches) from the tips of the ribs. Pull and cut off the layer of fat and meat between the line and the rib tips, to expose the ends of the bones (above).*

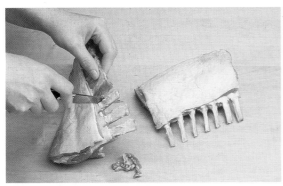 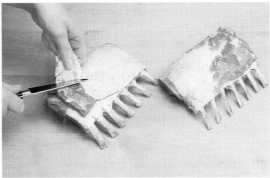

3 *CLEANING THE RIB TIPS. With a knife, cut out the meat and fat from between the bared rib ends (above); you can save these strips of meat to use in a stew. Holding each rack firmly, scrape the exposed bones with the knife to remove any remaining bits of meat and fat. Be careful not to split the fragile bones.*

4 *REMOVING EXCESS FAT. Holding the knife blade almost parallel with the meat, pare any excess fat from the meat.*

Preparing Noisettes from a Rack

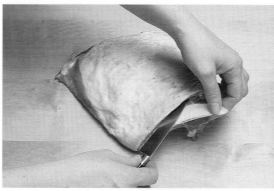

1 *REMOVING THE SHOULDER BLADE REMNANT. Place the rack, concave side down, on a wooden board. Slit open the shoulder end with a small pointed knife and cut out any remnant of the shoulder blade (above).*

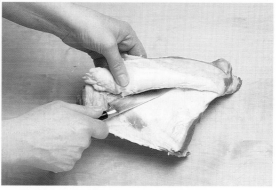

2 *STRIPPING OFF THE FAT. Insert the knife between the outer layer of fat and the lean meat. Keeping the blade as close to the meat as possible, work it to loosen the fat and the attached bark — the outer membrane — taking care not to cut into the flesh. Peel back the fat as you loosen it. Trim any remaining fat, keeping the knife blade parallel to the meat.*

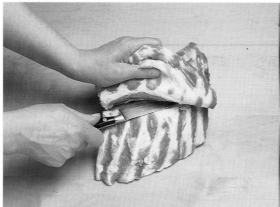

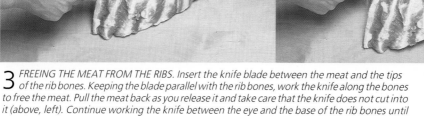

3 *FREEING THE MEAT FROM THE RIBS. Insert the knife blade between the meat and the tips of the rib bones. Keeping the blade parallel with the rib bones, work the knife along the bones to free the meat. Pull the meat back as you release it and take care that the knife does not cut into it (above, left). Continue working the knife between the eye and the base of the rib bones until the blade reaches the back bone (above, right).*

4 *CUTTING THE MEAT FROM THE BACKBONE. Turn the meat around, insert the blade between the eye and the backbone and cut the eye and attached flap of meat free (above). Then cut away the gristle from the eye.*

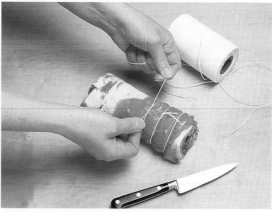

5 *ROLLING UP THE LAMB. Starting at the eye end, roll up the meat into a compact cylinder. Pull free about 90 cm (36 inches) of string and tie it around the meat at 2.5 cm (1 inch) intervals, cutting the string after each knot. Slice the meat into noisettes ready for cooking.*

Brown Stock

Makes about 3 litres (5 pints)
Working time: about 40 minutes
Total time: about 6 hours

1.5 kg	veal breast (or veal or beef shin), cut into 7.5 cm (3 inch) pieces	3 lb
1.5 kg	uncooked veal or beef bones, cracked	3 lb
2	onions, quartered	2
2	sticks celery, chopped	2
2	carrots, sliced	2
3	unpeeled garlic cloves, crushed	3
8	black peppercorns	8
3	cloves	3
2 tsp	fresh thyme, or ½ tsp dried thyme	2 tsp
1	bay leaf	1

Preheat the oven to 220°C (425°F or Mark 7). Place the meat, bones, onions, celery and carrots in a large roasting pan and roast them in the oven until they are well browned — about 1 hour. Transfer them to a stockpot. Pour ½ litre (16 fl oz) of water into the roasting pan, scrape up the browned bits from the bottom and add the liquid to the pot.

Add the garlic, peppercorns and cloves. Add enough water to cover the contents by about 7.5 cm (3 inches). Bring to the boil, then reduce to a slow simmer, and skim any impurities from the surface. Add the thyme and bay leaf, then simmer very gently for 4 hours, skimming occasionally. Strain and discard the solids. Allow the stock to stand until it is tepid, then refrigerate it overnight or freeze it long enough for the fat to congeal. Spoon off and discard the layer of fat.

Tightly covered and refrigerated, the stock may be safely kept for two or three days. Frozen, the stock may be kept for as long as six months.

EDITOR'S NOTE: Browning in the oven should produce a rich mahogany colour. If your stock does not seem dark enough, cook 1 tablespoon of tomato paste in a small pan over medium heat, stirring constantly, until it darkens — about 3 minutes. Add this to the stock about 1 hour before the end of cooking. Any combination of meat and bones may be used. Ask your butcher to crack the bones.

Chicken Stock

Makes about 2 litres (3½ pints)
Working time: about 20 minutes
Total time: about 4 hours

2.5 kg	uncooked chicken trimmings and bones, bones cracked with a heavy knife	5 lb
2	carrots, cut into 1 cm (½ inch) thick rounds	2
2	sticks celery, cut into 2.5 cm (1 inch) pieces	2
2	large onions (about 500 g/1 lb) cut in half, one half stuck with 2 cloves	2
2	fresh thyme sprigs, or ½ tsp dried thyme	2
1 or 2	bay leaves	1 or 2
10 to 15	parsley stems	10 to 15
5	black peppercorns	5

Put the chicken trimmings and bones into a heavy stockpot; pour in enough water to cover them by about 5 cm (2 inches). Bring the liquid to the boil over medium heat, skimming off the scum that rises to the surface. Reduce the heat and simmer the liquid for 10 minutes, skimming and adding a little cold water to help precipitate the scum.

Add the vegetables, herbs and peppercorns, and submerge them in the liquid. If necessary, pour in enough additional water to cover the contents of the pot. Simmer the stock for 2 to 3 hours, skimming as necessary to remove the scum.

Strain the stock and discard the solids. Allow the stock to stand until it is tepid, then refrigerate it overnight or freeze it long enough for the fat to congeal. Spoon off and discard the layer of fat.

Tightly covered and refrigerated, the stock may be safely kept for two or three days. Stored in small, tightly covered freezer containers and frozen, the stock may be kept for as long as six months.

EDITOR'S NOTE: The chicken gizzard and heart may be added to the stock. Wings and necks — rich in natural gelatine — produce a particularly gelatinous stock, ideal for sauces and jellied dishes. The liver should never be used for stock.

Glossary

Allspice: the dried berry of a member of the myrtle family. Used whole or ground, it is called allspice because its flavour resembles a combination of clove, cinnamon and nutmeg.

Arrowroot: a tasteless, starchy, white powder refined from the root of a tropical plant; it is used to thicken purées and sauces. Unlike flour, it becomes transparent when cooked.

Aspic: a clear savoury jelly made from reduced stock. It is used for coating meat, fish or vegetables, or for encasing them in decorative moulds.

Balsamic vinegar: a mild, extremely fragrant wine-based vinegar made in northern Italy. Traditionally, the vinegar is aged for at least seven years in a series of casks made of various woods.

Basil: a leafy herb with a strong, spicy aroma when fresh, often used in Italian cooking. Covered with olive oil and refrigerated in a tightly sealed container, fresh basil leaves may be kept for up to six months.

Baste: to help brown and flavour a food, and keep it from drying out, by pouring pan drippings or other liquid over it during cooking.

Batavian endive (also called escarole): a broad leaved green with a pleasantly bitter flavour, best used in combination with sweeter greens.

Bâtonnet (also called bâton): a vegetable piece that has been cut in the shape of a stick; bâtonnets are slightly larger than julienne.

Bay leaves: the aromatic leaves of *Laurus nobilis* — a Mediterranean evergreen — used fresh or dried to flavour stocks and stews; also available in powder form. Dried bay leaves when broken have very sharp edges and can injure internally, so they should be removed before serving.

Bean curd: (see Tofu).

Blanch: to partially cook food by briefly immersing it in boiling water. Blanching makes thin-skinned fruits and vegetables easier to peel; it can also mellow strong flavours.

Braise: to cook meat, vegetables or a combination of the two with some liquids over low heat. Braising can be done in the oven or on top of the stove. It helps to moisten and tenderize the food.

Broad beans: a European variety of bean with large seeds and thick pods, eaten fresh or dried. Except for the very youngest broad beans, only the seeds are edible and the maturer ones should also have their thin skins removed before cooking.

Buckwheat groats (also called kasha): the nutty-tasting seeds of the buckwheat plant, hulled, steamed, dried, and sometimes ground; often also toasted to intensify flavour.

Bulb fennel: see Fennel.

Burghul (also called bulgur): a type of cracked wheat, where the kernels are steamed and then dried before being crushed.

Calorie (or kilocalorie): a precise measure of the energy food supplies when it is broken down for use in the body.

Cardamom: the bittersweet, aromatic dried seeds or whole pods of a plant in the ginger family. Cardamom seeds may be used whole or ground.

Casserole: a heavy, heat-absorbing pot, ideal for cooking soups and stews slowly. To prevent evaporation of the liquid, the casserole should have a tight lid. Only fireproof casseroles made specially for the purpose should be used on top of the stove.

Caul: the fatty membrane that surrounds a pig's stomach. When wrapped round a lean minced-meat filling, it melts during cooking and moistens the meat.

Cayenne pepper: a fiery powder ground from the seeds and pods of red peppers. Used in small amounts to heighten other flavours.

Ceps (also called porcini): wild mushrooms with a pungent, earthy flavour that survives drying or long cooking. Dried ceps should be soaked in water before they are used.

Chervil: a lacy, slightly anise-flavoured herb often used as a companion to other herbs, such as tarragon and chives. Because long cooking may kill its flavour, chervil should be added at the last minute.

Chicory: a small, cigar-shaped vegetable, composed of many tightly wrapped white to pale-yellow leaves which have a pleasant bitter flavour.

Chili peppers: hot or mild red, yellow or green members of the pepper family. Fresh or dried, most chili peppers contain volatile oils that can irritate the skin and eyes; they must be handled carefully *(see caution, page 83)*.

Chine bone: the back bone.

Chinese cabbage (also called Chinese leaves): an elongated cabbage resembling cos lettuce, with long, broad ribs and crinkled, light green leaves.

Cholesterol: a waxlike substance that is manufactured in the human body and also found in foods of animal origin. Although a certain amount of cholesterol is necessary for proper body functioning, an excess can accumulate in the arteries, contributing to heart disease. See also Monounsaturated fats; Polyunsaturated fats; Saturated fats.

Concasse: a sauce of a crushed or chopped vegetable, usually tomato; from the French word for crush or chop.

Coriander (also called cilantro): the pungent, peppery leaves of the coriander plant or its earthy-tasting dried seeds. It is a common seasoning in Middle-Eastern, Oriental and Latin-American cookery.

Cornflour: a starchy, white powder made from corn kernels and used to thicken many puddings and sauces. Like arrowroot, it is transparent when cooked. When cooked conventionally, a liquid containing cornflour must be stirred constantly in the early stages to prevent lumps from forming.

Coulis: a sieved vegetable or fruit purée.

Couscous: a fine semolina grain, served with the classic North African stew of the same name.

Crème de cassis: a blackcurrant liqueur.

Crème fraîche: a slightly ripened, sharp-tasting french cream containing about 35% fat.

Cumin: the aromatic seeds of an umbelliferous plant similar to fennel, used whole or powdered as a spice, especially in Indian and Latin-American dishes. Toasting gives it a nutty flavour.

Deglaze: to dissolve the brown particles left in a pan after roasting or sautéing by stirring in wine, stock, water or cream.

Degrease: to remove the accumulated fat from stock or cooking liquid by skimming it off with a spoon or blotting it up with paper towels. To eliminate the last traces of fat, draw an ice cube through the warm liquid; the fat will cling to the cube.

Dijon mustard: a smooth mustard once manufactured only in Dijon, France; it may be flavoured with herbs, green peppercorns or wine.

Escalope: in this volume, an adaptation of the traditional veal escalope. A thin slice of lean lamb is cut from the fillet end of the leg, then flattened out and tenderized with a mallet before frying or grilling.

Eye of meat: the tender strip of lean meat from best end of neck. Also the larger of the two tender strips that make up a loin (the other strip is the fillet).

Fat: a basic component of many foods, comprising three types of fatty acid — saturated, monounsaturated and polyunsaturated — in varying proportions. See also Monounsaturated fats; Polyunsaturated fats; Saturated fats.

Fennel: a herb (also called wild fennel) whose feathery leaves and dried seeds have a mild anise flavour and are much used for flavouring. Its vegetable relative, the bulb — or Florence — fennel (also called finocchio) — can be eaten raw in salads or cooked.

Fenugreek: a plant native to Asia. The seeds are highly aromatic with a bitter aftertaste and are normally used as a flavouring in Indian cookery.

Fermented black beans: soya beans that have been cured in salt; sometimes with citrus peel; used in Chinese dishes. To remove their excess salt, rinse the beans before use.

Feta cheese: a salty Greek and Middle Eastern cheese made from goat's or sheep's milk. The curds are ripened in their own salted whey.

Fillet: the most tender muscle in the lamb's carcass, located inside the loin.

Five-spice powder: a pungent blend of ground Sichuan pepper, star anise, cassia, cloves and fennel seeds; available in Asian food shops.

Fromage frais: a soft, smooth cheese made from skimmed milk. The *fromage frais* used in this book includes a small proportion of added cream and has an 8 per cent fat content.

Ginger: the spicy, buff-coloured rhizome, or rootlike stem, of the ginger plant, used as a seasoning either in fresh form or dried and powdered. Dried ginger makes a poor substitute for fresh ginger root.

Gratin: a baked dish with a crunchy topping of breadcrumbs or grated cheese browned in the oven or under the grill.

Green peppercorns: the green, unripened berries from the pepper vine. Sold fresh, dried or preserved in brine, the same berries are used to make black, red and white pepper.

Hazelnut: the fruit of a shrublike tree found primarily in Turkey, Italy and Spain, and in the United States.

Horseradish: a plant native to Eastern Europe and Asia. Its cylindrical root is grated for use as a pungent flavouring.

Julienne: the French term for vegetables or other food cut into fine strips.

Juniper berries: the berries of the juniper tree, used as the key flavouring in gin. They lend a resinous tang to marinades and sauces.

Kasha: see Buckwheat groats.

Kohlrabi: a cruciferous vegetable with an enlarged stem in the form of a light-green or lavender bulb.

Madeira: a fortified wine from the island of Madeira. It has an underlying burnt flavour, which is the result of heating the wine after fermentation.

Mange-tout: flat green pea pods eaten whole, with only stems and strings removed.

Mango: a fruit grown throughout the tropics, with sweet, succulent, yellow-orange flesh that is extremely rich in vitamin A. It may cause an allergic reaction in some individuals.

Marinade: a mixture of aromatic ingredients in which meat is allowed to stand before cooking to enrich its flavour. Some marinades will tenderize meat, but they do not penetrate deeply.

Medallion: in lamb cookery, a round or oval slice of lean lamb, for frying or grilling.

Mirin: a sweet Japanese cooking wine that is made from rice. If mirin is unavailable, substitute white wine or sake mixed with a little sugar.

Mixed spices: a mixture of spices and herbs, including several of the following: nutmeg, mace, cinnamon, cayenne pepper, white pepper, cloves, ground bay leaf, thyme, marjoram and savory.

Monounsaturated fats: one of the three types of fats found in foods. Monounsaturated fats are believed not to raise the level of cholesterol in the blood.

Morels: wild mushrooms with brown, pitted caps. Dried morels should be soaked in water before use.

Mozzarella: a soft kneaded cheese from southern Italy, traditionally made from buffalo's milk, but now also made from cow's milk. Full-fat mozzarella has a fat content of 40 to 50 per cent, but lower-fat versions are available. The low-fat mozzarella used in the recipes in this book has a fat content of only about 16 per cent.

Noisettes: boned lamb from the best end of neck or loin rolled, tied and cut into rounds for grilling or frying.

Non-reactive pan: a cooking vessel whose surface does not chemically react with food. This includes stainless steel, enamel, glass and some alloys. Untreated cast iron and aluminium may react with acids, producing discoloration or a peculiar taste.

Nori: paper-like dark green or black sheets of dried seaweed, often used in Japanese cuisine as a flavouring or as wrappers for rice and vegetables.

Okra: the green pods of a plant indigenous to Africa, where it is called gumbo. In stews, okra is prized for its thickening properties.

Olive oil: any of various grades of oil extracted from olives. Extra virgin olive oil, which has a full, fruity flavour and the lowest acidity level, and virgin olive oil come from the first pressing of the olives. Pure olive oil, a processed blend of olive oils, has the lightest taste and the highest acidity.

Paprika: a slightly sweet, spicy, bright-red powder produced by grinding dried red peppers. The best type of paprika is Hungarian.

Passata: the sieved flesh of ripe red tomatoes, available bottled from delicatessens or large supermarkets.

Paupiettes: very thin slices of meat, which have been stuffed and rolled.

Pernod: an anise-flavoured spirit made in France.

Phyllo pastry: a paper-thin flour-and-water pastry popular in Greece and the Middle East. It can be bought, fresh or frozen, from delicatessens and shops specializing in Middle-Eastern food.

Pilaff: a dish of rice or other grains, which is heated first in a little oil, then simmered in water or stock. Meat or vegetables are often added to turn a pilaff into a main course.

Pine-nuts: seeds from the cones of the stone pine, a tree native to the Mediterranean. Toasting brings out their buttery flavour.

Poach: to cook gently in simmering liquid. The temperature of the poaching liquid should be approximately 90°C (200°F), and its surface should merely tremble.

Polyunsaturated fats: one of the three types of fats found in foods. They exist in abundance in such vegetable oils as safflower, sunflower, corn and soya. Polyunsaturated fats lower the level of cholesterol in the blood.

Pomegranate: a red-skinned fruit with succulent edible seeds, which are picked out and eaten; the bitter white membranes are discarded. Pomegranates are in season in the autumn.

Porcini: (see Ceps)

Prosciutto: an uncooked, dry-cured and slightly salty Italian ham, sliced paper-thin.

Purée: to reduce food to a smooth, even, pulplike consistency by mashing it, passing it through a sieve, or processing it in a food processor or a blender.

Reduce: to boil down a liquid in order to concentrate its flavour and thicken its consistency.

Refresh: to rinse a briefly cooked vegetable under cold water to arrest its cooking and set its colour.

Rice vinegar: a mild, fragrant vinegar that is less assertive than cider vinegar or distilled white vinegar. It is available in dark, light, seasoned and sweetened varieties; Japanese rice vinegar generally is milder than the Chinese version.

Rice wine: Chinese rice wine (*shao-hsing*) is brewed from rice and wine. Japanese rice wine (sake) has a different flavour but may be used as a substitute. If rice wine is not available, use sherry in its place.

Saddle: a roasting joint consisting of a pair of whole loins. A ''long'' saddle includes the pair of chump ends and sometimes the kidneys and tail as well as the loins.

Safflower oil: a vegetable oil that contains the highest proportion of polyunsaturated fats.

Saffron: the dried yellowish-red stigmas of the crocus flower, saffron yields a pungent flavour and a bright yellow colour. It is available both in thread and in powdered form.

Sake: See Rice wine.

Salsify: a slender, tapering root, about twice the length of a carrot, with a white or yellowish skin and a faint oysterish flavour. See also Scorzonera.

Saturated fats: one of the three types of fats found in foods. They exist in abundance in animal products and coconut and palm oils; they raise the level of cholesterol in the blood. Because high blood-cholesterol levels may cause heart disease, saturated fat consumption should be restricted to less than 15 per cent of the calories provided by the daily diet.

Sauté: to cook a food quickly in a small amount of hot fat, usually in an uncovered frying pan.

Sear: to brown meat by exposing it briefly to very high heat, sealing in natural juices.

Sesame oil: an oil derived from the seed of the sesame plant, frequently used in Chinese cooking.

Shallot: a refined cousin of the onion, with a subtle flavour and papery, red-brown skin.

Shank: the lower end of a leg. The fore-shank, or knuckle, is the equivalent cut from a shoulder.

Shiitake mushrooms: a variety of mushroom, originally grown only in Japan, sold fresh or dried. The dried form should be soaked and stemmed before use.

Shoyu: see Soy sauce.

Sichuan pepper (also called Chinese pepper, Japanese pepper or anise pepper): a dried shrub berry with a tart, aromatic flavour that is less piquant than black pepper.

Simmer: to maintain a liquid at a temperature just below its boiling point so that the liquid's surface barely ripples.

Skimmed milk: milk from which almost all the fat has been removed.

Sodium: a nutrient essential to maintaining the proper balance of fluids in the body. In most diets, a major source of the element is table salt, which contains 40 per cent sodium. Excess sodium may contribute to high blood pressure, which increases the risk of heart disease. One teaspoon (5.5 g) of salt, with 2,132 milligrams of sodium, contains just over the maximum daily amount recommended by the World Health Organization.

Soy sauce: a savoury, salty brown liquid made from fermented soya beans and available in both light and dark versions. One tablespoon of ordinary soy sauce contains 1,030 milligrams of sodium; lower-sodium variations, such as naturally fermented shoyu, used in the recipes in this book, may contain half that amount.

Star anise: a woody, star-shaped spice, similar in flavour to anise. Ground star anise is a component of five-spice powder.

Steam: to cook food in the steam created by a boiling liquid. The food is placed in a covered container with a perforated base through which the steam rises from the liquid below. Steaming vegetables preserves the vitamins and flavours that are ordinarily lost in boiling.

Stir-fry: to cook cubes or strips of meat or vegetables, or a combination of both, over high heat in a small amount of oil, stirring constantly to ensure even cooking in a short time. The traditional cooking vessel is a Chinese wok; a heavy frying pan may also be used for stir-frying.

Stock: a savoury liquid prepared by simmering meat, bones, trimming, aromatic vegetables, herbs and spices in water. Stock forms a flavour-rich base for sauces and stews.

Sun-dried tomatoes: tomatoes that have been dried in the open air to concentrate their flavour; some are then packed in oil. Most sun-dried tomatoes are of Italian origin.

Tabasco sauce: a hot, unsweetened chili sauce. A similar Asian version is the Thai *sriracha* sauce.

Tahini (also called sesame paste): a nutty-tasting paste made from ground sesame seeds that are usually roasted.

Tarragon: a strong herb with a sweet anise taste. In combination with other herbs — especially rosemary, sage or thyme — it should be used sparingly, to avoid a clash of flavours. Because heat intensifies tarragon's flavour, cooked dishes require smaller amounts.

Thyme: a versatile herb with a zesty, slightly fruity flavour and strong aroma.

Timbale: a creamy mixture of vegetables or meat baked in a mould. The term, French for "kettledrum" also denotes a drum-shaped baking dish.

Tofu (also called bean curd): a dense, unfermented soya bean product with a mild flavour. It is rich in protein, relatively low in calories and free of cholesterol. Lightly pressed silken tofu is used for blending into other ingredients; heavily pressed firm tofu, which has a texture similar to cheese, may be cubed or sliced. Soft tofu, with a texture midway between the two, is also available.

Tomato paste: a concentrated tomato purée, available in cans and tubes, used in sauces and soups. See also Tomato purée.

Tomato purée: a purée made from skinned fresh or canned tomatoes. Available commercially, but should not be confused with the thicker, concentrated tomato paste sometimes labelled tomato purée.

Total fat: an individual's daily intake of polyunsaturated, monounsaturated and saturated fats. Nutritionists recommend that total fat constitute no more than 35 per cent of the energy in the diet. The term as used in this book refers to the combined fats in a given dish or food.

Turmeric: a spice used as a colouring agent and occasionally as a substitute for saffron. It has a musty odour and a slightly bitter flavour.

Vine leaves: the tender, lightly flavoured leaves of the grapevine, used in many ethnic cuisines as wrappers for savoury mixtures. They are sold fresh or preserved in brine, in which case they should be soaked and rinsed in several changes of water to eliminate the salt.

Virgin olive oil: see Olive oil.

Water chestnut: the walnut-sized tuber of an aquatic Asian plant, with rough brown skin and white, sweet, crisp flesh. Fresh water chestnuts may be refrigerated for up to two weeks; they must be peeled before use. To store canned water chestnuts, first blanch or rinse them, then refrigerate for up to three weeks in fresh water changed daily. Jerusalem artichoke makes an acceptable substitute.

White pepper: a powder ground from the same dried berry as that used to make black pepper. Unlike black pepper, the berries are allowed to ripen and are ground without their shells. Used as a less visible alternative to black pepper in light-coloured foods.

Wild rice: the seeds of a water grass native to the Great Lakes region of the United States. Wild rice is appreciated for its robust flavour.

Worcester sauce: a hot sauce containing vinegar, molasses, chili peppers and tropical fruits and spices. The version used in this book contains no sugar and no added salt.

Yellow bean sauce: a sauce made from fermented yellow soya beans. It is available from most Chinese grocery shops.

Yogurt: a smooth-textured, semi-solid cultured milk product. Low-fat yogurt contains about 1 per cent fat. Greek yogurt, which is made from full-cream milk, has a 10 per cent fat content.

Index

Picture Credits

Cover: Chris Knaggs. 4: top, Chris Knaggs; left, Andrew Whittuck; bottom, Ian O'Leary. 5: top left, Graham Kirk; top right, Andrew Whittuck; bottom, John Elliott. 6: David Johnson. 9: art by Ian Bott, London. 10-11: Chris Knaggs. 12: Ian O'Leary. 13: Chris Knaggs. 14: Graham Kirk. 15: Andrew Whittuck. 16: Renée Comet. 17: John Elliott. 18: Graham Kirk. 19-20: Renée Comet. 21: Andrew Whittuck. 22: Jan Baldwin. 23: Chris Knaggs. 24: top, Ian O'Leary; bottom, John Elliott. 25: John Elliott. 26: Ian O'Leary. 27: Renée Comet. 28: Chris Knaggs. 29: Graham Kirk. 30-31: Ian O'Leary. 32: top, Graham Kirk; bottom, John Elliott. 33: Chris Knaggs. 34: Renée Comet. 35: Graham Kirk. 36-37: Renée Comet. 38: John Elliott. 39: Andrew Whittuck. 40-41: Renée Comet. 42: Jan Baldwin. 43: top, Ian O'Leary; bottom, John Elliott. 44: Jan Baldwin. 45: John Elliott. 46-49: Renée Comet. 50: Andrew Whittuck. 51: Chris Knaggs. 52-54: John Elliott. 55: Graham Kirk. 56-57: John Elliott. 58: Chris Knaggs. 59: Andrew Whittuck. 60-61: Ian O'Leary. 62-63: Renée Comet. 64-65: Chris Knaggs. 66-67: Ian O'Leary. 68: Graham Kirk. 69: Ian O'Leary. 70-71: Graham Kirk. 72: Jan Baldwin. 73-74: Renée Comet. 75: Graham Kirk. 76-77: Jan Baldwin. 78-79: Renée Comet. 80: Ian O'Leary. 81-82: Renée Comet. 83: Chris Knaggs. 84: Ian O'Leary. 85: Renée Comet. 87-89: Chris Knaggs. 90: John Elliott. 91: Ian O'Leary. 92-93: Renée Comet. 95: Graham Kirk. 96: Jan Baldwin. 97: Andrew Whittuck. 98: Jan Baldwin. 99: Renée Comet. 100: Chris Knaggs. 101-102: Andrew Whittuck. 103-104: Chris Knaggs. 105: Jan Baldwin. 106-107: Andrew Whittuck. 108: John Elliott. 109: Andrew Whittuck. 110: Renée Comet. 111-112: Chris Knaggs. 113: Jan Baldwin. 114: Chris Knaggs. 115: Jan Baldwin. 116: Graham Kirk. 117: Chris Knaggs. 118: top, Renée Comet; right, John Elliott. 119: Andrew Whittuck. 120-121: Chris Knaggs. 122: Graham Kirk. 124: Ian O'Leary. 125-127: Renée Comet. 128: Jan Baldwin. 129: Chris Knaggs. 130-131: Andrew Whittuck. 132: John Elliott. 133: Ian O'Leary. 134-136: John Elliott.

Props: the editors wish to thank the following outlets and manufacturers; all are based in London unless otherwise stated. 16: Ginza 'Things Japanese', Washington D.C. 19: Joan Tapper, U.S.A. 20: Cobweb, New York. 24: napkin, Ewart Liddell. 26: napkin, Kilkenny. 30: platter (top), Thomas (London) Ltd.; platter (bottom), Inshop. 32: cloth, Ewart Liddell. 34: napkin, Kilkenny. 36: Williams-Sonoma, Washington D.C. 37: China Closet, Kensington, Md., U.S.A. 40: Steven Hill, Kansas City, Mo., U.S.A. 41: Stephen Kilborn, Jackie Chalkley; bowl, Ron Bower, Jackie Chalkley, Washington D.C. 43: marble, W.E. Grant & Co. (Marble) Ltd.; 47: Sandra Selesnick, Full Circle, Alexandria, Virginia, U.S.A. 48: background, Michael Latil, U.S.A. 54: marble, W.E. Grant & Co (Marble) Ltd. 55: carvers, Mappin & Webb Silversmiths. 58: cloth, Ewart Liddell. 59: plate, Rosenthal (London) Ltd.; cloth, Ewart Liddell. 62: plate, Preferred Stock, Washington D.C.; bowl, The Flower Designer, Washington D.C.; placemat and napkin, Abrielle Fine Linens & Lingerie, Washington D.C. 63: plates, Gwathmey/Siegel for Sind, Powell and Alessi, U.S.A.; bowl, The American Hand Plus, Washington D.C. 68: rice dish, Mary Wondraush; large dish, Derek Emms, The Craftsmen Potters Shop. 72: plate, Hutschenreuther (U.K.) Ltd. 73: Cobweb, New York. 74: Ruff & Ready Furnishings, Washington D.C. 75: napkin, Kilkenny; cloth, Ewart Liddell; knife and fork, Mappin & Webb Silversmiths. 76: marble, W.E. Grant & Co. (Marble) Ltd. 77: plates, Villeroy & Boch; napkin, Ewart Liddell. 78: Peter Kaizer, The American Hand Plus, U.S.A. 84: rice dish, Tony Gant; large dish, Winchcombe Pottery, The Craftsmen Potters Shop. 92: bowls, Nora Pate Studio, San Francisco, Calif. 93: Cobweb, New York. 95: plate, The Reject China Shop. 96: plate, Royal Worcester, Worcester. 97: pie dish, Winchcombe Pottery, The Craftsmen Potters Shop. 98: china, Inshop. 99: Sasaki Crystal, Inc., New York. 103-104, 109: marble, W.E. Grant & Co. (Marble) Ltd. 117: fork, Mappin & Webb Silversmiths. 127: WILTON Armetale, New York. 132: plate, Tony Gant; pie dish, Mike Dodd, The Craftsmen Potters Shop. 133: salad bowl, Clive Bowen, The Craftsmen Potters Shop.

Acknowledgements

The index for this book was prepared by Myra Clark, London. The editors also wish to thank: I.A. Bell and O. Kadlecek, Wiener Porzellanmanufaktur Augarten, Gesellschaft MBH, Vienna, Austria; Paul van Biene, London; René Bloom, London; Maureen Burrows, London; David Donaldson, ADAS, Chichester, Sussex; Jonathan Driver, London; Wendy Gibbons, London; Bruce Horn, Hellet's Butchers, Kimbolton, Huntingdon; Lidgates of Holland Park, London; Meat & Livestock Commission, Milton Keynes; Perstorp Warerite Ltd., London; Sharp Electronics (U.K.) Ltd., London; Jane Stevenson, London; Toshiba (U.K.) Ltd., London.

Colour separations by Fotolitomec, S.N.C., Milan, Italy
Typesetting by G. Beard & Son Ltd., Brighton, Sussex, England
Printed and bound by Wing King Tong, Hong Kong.